SEAL-FOLK
AND OCEAN PADDLERS

Sliochd nan Ròn

John M. MacAulay

Illustrations by
Venessa Wingad

The White Horse Press

© 1998 John M. MacAulay
"Fernhaven"
Flodabay, Isle of Harris,
Outer Hebrides, HS3 3HA
Tel. 01859 530 340

First published 1998 by The White Horse Press
10 High Street, Knapwell, Cambridge CB3 8NR
and
1 Strond, Isle of Harris, HS5 3UD

All rights reserved

Set in 10 on 12 point Bookman

Printed in Great Britain by Biddles Ltd, Guildford

398
.21
McA
840777

ISBN 1-874267-39-1

A catalogue record for this book is available from the British Library

For Catherine and Lorna

About the author

John MacAulay (fifty-seven) is a writer and historian who now concentrates his efforts on researching the cultural links between the Hebrideans and the Norse. A former shipwright and charter yacht skipper, this native Hebridean who is a fluent Gaelic speaker is well equipped for the task. Born to a crofting/fishing family on the Isle of Harris, and brought up during a time when oral tradition and folklore had not yet succumbed to the pressures of modern society, he now recalls the wealth of information imparted by a people to whom 'heritage' was an element of daily life. Living with his wife Cathy on the family croft (their two daughters live on the mainland) he enjoys the isolation and closeness to nature which island life affords. He is the author of a history of Rodel Church, *Silent Tower* (Pentland Press, 1993), and of *Birlinn: Longships of the Hebrides* (White Horse Press, 1996).

CONTENTS

Foreword by Tony Ford — xi

Preface — xvii

Seal-folk — 1

Champion of Champions — 10

Hebridean and Norse Tradition — 15

Mythology, Fantasy — 32

Recorded Events — 55

Kayaks — 74

Lapp of honour — 98

References and Bibliography — 107

A note on Sources

My quest for the Seal-folk has led me to many writers of the nineteenth and early twentieth centuries, who are not much in fashion today. They include immensely learned folklorists like Kauffman and Blind, and energetic and observant travellers like Baron von Duben and Captain Thomas. I believe we should now give a second hearing to their 'ethnological fancies'. They travelled and researched in a world where there was far less dilution of ethnic cultures and oral traditions than we can experience today: we should allow, then, that they might have started with certain insights that would be nigh impossible for modern students, even though their methods might not always meet our current scientific criteria.

I owe a special mention to David MacRitchie. The youngest son of a surgeon with the East India Company, born on the sixteenth of April 1851, he was a Fellow of the Society of Antiquaries of Scotland and Ireland, and a Fellow of the Royal Anthropological Institute of Great Britain and Ireland. He was also one of the founder members of the St Andrew Society, Edinburgh, the aim of which is to define Scotland's position in history. He was the author of various ethnographic and antiquarian works, including *The Testimony of Tradition*, *Fians, Fairies and Picts*, *Scottish Gypsies Under the Stewarts* and *The Savages of Gaelic Tradition*. David MacRitchie, who contributed so much to our knowledge and understanding of traditional lore, died on the fourteenth of January 1925.

A little over one hundred years ago he was obviously giving close consideration to the the subject of 'Finfolk' and kayaks, with his several contributions to magazines and scientific journals, linking reality to folklore. His work in this area has been largely misunderstood, and even openly scorned. It now forms the backbone of my attempt to continue this task of shedding light on the maritime mystery of the 'seal-folk'. I unashamedly endorse his expertise and diligence in pursuing this particular line of investigation, in the hope that others may also be stimulated and encouraged to follow similarily oblique lines of study in traditions and culture.

Acknowledgements

This book is the result of a chance encounter with a school teacher from Norway who was on holiday on the Isle of Harris. I am deeply indebted to Britt Sneltvedt for introducing me to one part of North Norwegian culture that I was previously unaware of, which combined with her curiosity and interest in Hebridean folklore gave me the idea for writing about our perplexing legends of the seal-folk.

Since then there have been quite a number of interesting individuals in diverse capacities who have assisted and encouraged me, and I am extremely grateful to all of them. They provided the stimulus and the incentive to continue; and collectively, they are responsible for the creation of this book – errors and inferences are all mine.

My special thanks to Robert Eaves and the ever helpful staff of Western Isles Libraries who have always managed to locate quickly whatever obscure material I requested; Charles Hunt (Curator of Marischal Museum, University of Aberdeen); Briony Crozier (Royal Museum of Scotland); Michael J.H. Westcott (Administrative Fellow, The University of Edinburgh); Duncan Rice (Principal and Vice Chancellor, University of Aberdeen) for his warm welcome and introduction; Colin Maclaren and library staff (Queen Mother Library and the Special Collections, King's College, University of Aberdeen); Alexander Adam (Aberdeen Medico-Chirurgical Society); E.J.Russell (The Corporation of The Hull Trinity House, Hull); Tony Ford (Organiser, Research and Newsletter Editor, The Historic Canoe and Kayak Association, St. Andreasberg); Einar Niemi

(Universitetet i Tromso); Alastair McIntosh (Centre for Human Ecology, Edinburgh); Lachlan Alick MacInnes (Leicester); Venessa Wingad (Black Cat Studio, Harris).

Furthermore, I would add that absolutely no disrespect is intended or implied in the use of the terms 'Finn' and 'Lapp' in reference to the Sami people. If anything at all, the opposite is true, and I am quite certain that the indigenous people of Orkney, Shetland, and the Hebrides, would find much in common with those folks whose maritime traditions and culture closely resembled their own, even up to fairly recent times.

Once more I am indebted to my publishers, Andrew and Alison Johnson, for their valued help and encouragement.

FOREWORD

Tony Ford FRGS
The Historic Canoe & Kayak Association

When my interest in the history of canoeing and kayaking first awakened, it was naively assumed that historians, ethnologists and marine archaeologists had documented all there was to learn, with types of craft, dates, and development of these craft all fixed in spatiogeographic terms. I now realise that this was a totally false assumption, and that the deeper one delves into any specific aspect of the history of small craft development and use, the greater the difficulty. I therefore welcome the publication of *Seal-folk and Ocean Paddlers* to add to the debate.

That Scotland and its outlying islands have been influenced by a number of cultures is accepted; nevertheless, we are left with a number of mysteries as to dates, events and material culture that cannot be fully explained. Among such issues is the folklore concerning Finn-folk, Seal-folk or Selkies, and the Kayak Men. Who were these people and where did they come from? Are we dealing with mistaken identity about two or more peoples, or are the names interchangeable? And do we accept the stories which have been handed down from generation to generation as fact, or only as folk tale?

John Macaulay is to be congratulated for his attempt to assemble historical records and to throw light on all these and other issues. He takes a different line of approach to the problem from my own: to him, the people are paramount in his search for an answer, whereas my own approach is to look at what is known of the craft. Is it possible that decked skin boats were used to journey between Norway and Scotland?

Reliance upon the internal combustion engine and other technical developments of the twentieth century sometimes alienates us from the achievements of our forefathers. Could anyone have crossed these northern waters, surviving maybe six days at sea in such a frail craft as a skin boat? In our present time we would perhaps dismiss such a feat as impossible. But who is to say that it was not achievable with skills and knowledge we have lost in our dependence on technology?

A major drawback of skin boats is that continuous use in the water cannot usually be for more than three days. If oil is not applied, osmosis – where water from outside is drawn through the hide – takes place. We know that the peoples living on either side of the Bering Sea frequently crossed in skin kayaks to war or trade with the other side – but the journey had to be made in three days or less. On the other hand, it is said the Irish curraghs were sailed to Iceland and possibly further west. The journey to Iceland would take at least five days, using the Gulf Stream and North Atlantic Drift. Here, the problem of osmosis was solved by tanning the hides in oak bark and soaking the skins in wool fat, a process recently replicated successfully by Tim Severin, as described in *The Brendan Voyage*.

One of the problems of research into historical skin boats is that the frames are of thin strips of wood or withies, and therefore when buried or abandoned, little evidence of their existence remains after a few centuries. There are also cultural limiting factors on skin boats, which tend to be constructed where timber is scarce, where there are no harbours, where there is heavy surf, or where portage requirements demand a light craft. It is believed they had their origins in southeast Europe and spread out in all directions from there, except Africa. There is evidence of skin boats of antiquity in Norway and elsewhere in Europe. They were also used in Britain and Ireland.

Now we come to the particular type of decked skin boat known as a kayak. This was a development of the Inuit, reaching Greenland somewhere between seven and eleven hundred years ago. There is no evidence that any culture other than the Inuit/Aleut possessed decked single, double or triple hole skin boats – i.e. what are known as kayaks. So should any connection between the Sjø-Sami, the 'Seal-folk', and kayak use be discounted?

There have been crossings in modern times of both the Atlantic and the Pacific Oceans in kayaks, so we should not dismiss the use of one man craft of relatively small dimensions being used to navigate large tracts of water. Then, too, recent archaeological finds along the Arctic coast of Russia include boat remains, and these could mean that our thinking about the development and distribution of watercraft along Arctic shores may need to be amended.

Kayaks, with or without their occupants, were certainly found off Scottish coasts. Ocean currents would not work in favour of an east going Atlantic crossing unless one started off the Newfoundland shore. There is also a theory that kayaks could be blown across the Atlantic by storms: here one wonders about human ability to weather a storm capable of blowing a kayak over one thousand miles. It is, however, known that whalers often took, forcibly or otherwise, 'Eskimos' and their kayaks on board their ships, and brought them back to Europe to 'exhibit'. A law was eventually passed prohibiting Dutch whalers from so doing. The presence of kayaks off Scotland is usually explained by ditchings or escapees from the whaling ships. This may be part answer: but can we be sure it is the whole one? Further research would be needed to establish any connection between dates of kayak landings on the Scottish coast and dates and routes of returning whaling fleets.

The Sjø-Sami (coastal Lapps) of Northern Norway have inhabited the fjords of the Norwegian coast for a thousand years or more. From early accounts, they are described as excellent boat builders and seafarers. They were expert whale and seal hunters, and used the typical circumpolar harpoons and other equipment. But there is no evidence that they used skin boats as did the other Arctic peoples. Their known craft were made of planks sewn together with sinews or plant roots, and these were considered so good that until quite recently neighbouring Norwegians often bought them. However, the inland cousins of the coastal Lapps did possess skin boats, easily transportable and easily portaged, which they used for river and lake crossing, fishing, and probably hunting. Here, then, is a thread on which one might dare to hang a theory. The peoples of Northern Norway had skin boats. Could they have been of the kayak type? Did they use them to cross to Scotland? Did some of them settle there, and could their presence explain the persistent tradition of 'Seal-folk'?

The Celts' main thrust of intercourse with Western Scotland came from Ireland and and a wealth of Celtic material has been found in Norway. There appear, then, to be strong commercial or other ties between the three wide flung locations. T.C. Lethbridge in *Herdsmen and Hermits – Celtic Seafarers in the Northern Seas* makes reference to Finn's spearmen who came across from Ireland, possibly in skin curraghs. It is interesting to note that the people of Ireland who used curraghs referred to them as 'canoes'. Here I should add that a kayak is a canoe, but a canoe is not necessarily a kayak, and it is on this basis that incorrect claims or assumptions have been made. But could Finn's men and Finn men (as the kayakers sighted off Scottish coasts were often called) be one and the same?

Where does all this take us? That voyages between the two distant shores of Norway and Scotland were made there can be no doubt. Personally, I would settle with a theory that the kayak finds on the Scottish coast got there via the whaling fleets, and that the Sjø-Sami reached Scotland, and perhaps the west coast of Ireland, in sewn planked boats. But other readers will have other theories: John Macaulay has laid the debate wide open, and we can be sure that *Seal-folk and Ocean Paddlers* will not be the final word on the subject. It reopens one of the most fascinating puzzles of Scottish maritime history, and leaves us with as many questions as answers. It is perhaps only right that this should be so, and that the mystery surrounding the Seal-folk of legend should remain.

Am Kurpark 4
37444 St Andreasberg
Germany

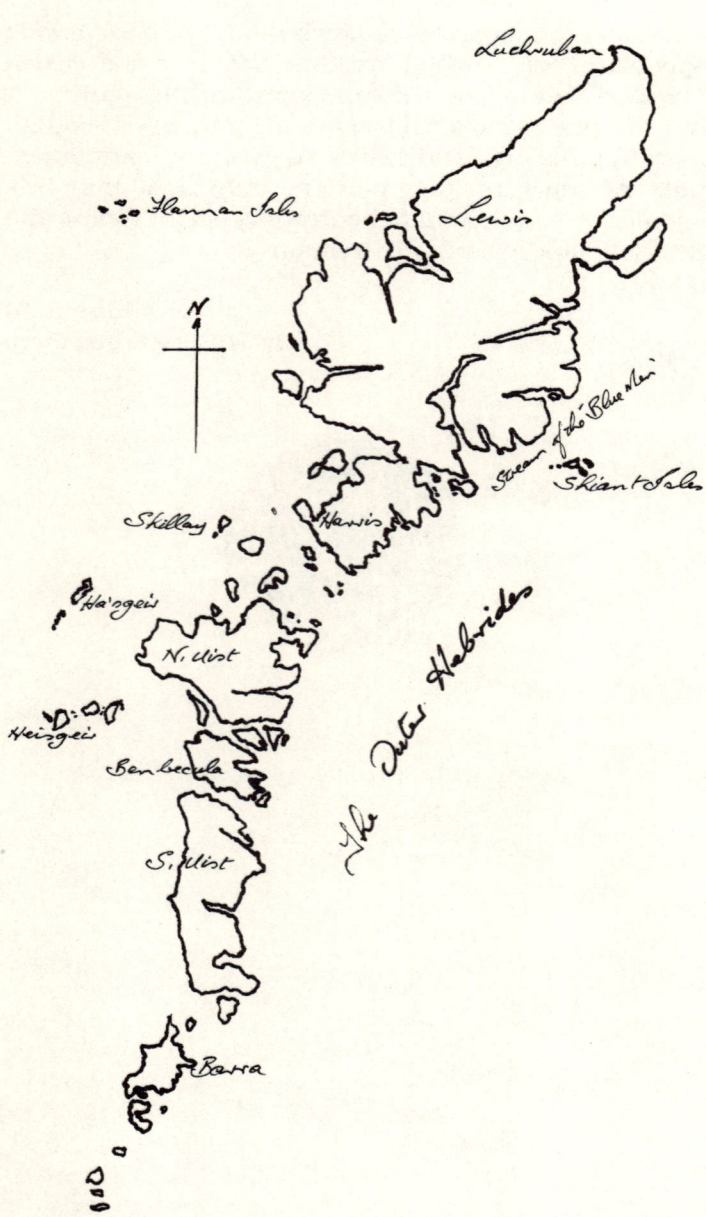

PREFACE

Boyhood on the rocky coast of the Hebrides naturally involved a close interaction with the marine environment. One learned to respect, not only the sea, but also what lived and moved upon and within it. The sea was partly our home. Even more so, possibly, than the island itself – all my forebears had lived in close harmony with the sea, reaping its bountiful harvest, partly of necessity, but mostly to satisfy the powerful yearning in the heart of the Hebridean to be at one with the very life-blood of Creation.

On long winter evenings gathered around the fireside, with both family and neighbours sharing in this domestic tranquility and safely sheltered from external uncertainties, we were introduced to the world of strange creatures of the sea: mermaids, seal-folk, and close encounters in 'the stream of the blue men' – *Sruth na Fir Ghorm* – and there are many gripping accounts of inexplicable events in the history of men and boats in these terrible tide-races where the ocean appears to have gone totally berserk.

Years later, I was to recall the story of the MacCodrum family (*sliochd nan ròn)* for the benefit of Britt Sneltvedt, on holiday from Norway. Explaining how they claimed, not only descent from the seals, but also from the Kings of Norway, I was careful to relate every detail as well as I could remember from the older fishermen of Grimsay, with whom, years ago, I was privileged to share a season at the lobster fishing on Heisgeir – the Monach Isles. I told Britt how I found it hard to accept that anyone could exist on the barren rocks and islets – the home of *sliochd nan ròn,* the seal-folk – to the west of the Hebrides, where they would be exposed to the full fury of the Atlantic Ocean.

Britt, in turn, explained her interest in the history of the Sjø-Sami folk – the Sea Sami or coastal Lapps of Northern Norway and its offshore islands. She told me

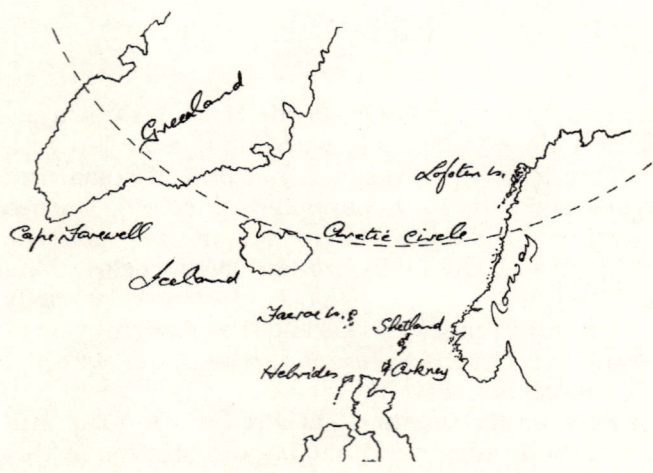

how these people survived quite comfortably in conditions where 'normal' people could not. Their home was the sea, and the sea provided all their needs. They had adapted to this form of existence and were quite independent of all other human requirements. 'What else could they possibly need?' Britt asked convincingly. I realised only then that there was an element of truth in the stories of long ago – *sliochd nan ròn* were alive, and proving to be very real people. Britt had provided that conceivable link, something I had not been particularily looking for, but yet, something I can now share with those who, like me, are deeply intrigued by the mysteries of the marine world.

~ 1 ~

SEAL-FOLK

> Stuff that the public won't believe aren't facts
>
> H.G. Wells, *The Sea Lady*

To claim direct descent from the seals is surely a recipe for instant ridicule, yet in the Hebrides there have been families who unashamedly acknowledged this curious aspect of their pedigree, in fact they were quite proud of it. Indeed the same is true of the Shetland and Orkney people, many of whom would readily testify to this astonishing tradition. Even on the west coast and islands of Ireland there are family names which still clearly indicate their association with the seals.

There is no longer a single person of the name MacCodrum left in North Uist, although there are some descendants of that family living whose forebears, like so many other islanders, had emigrated across the Atlantic to Cape Breton. The MacCodrums were a sept of the clan Ranald of the Isles, who were also of Norse origin, and supposedly had the peculiar characteristic of being descended from the seals. The story goes that they were seals by day, and only at night did they assume human form.

The best known member of this family was the bard John MacCodrum, commonly known by his patronymic Iain Mac Fhearchuir, who was born in North Uist around 1693, and is credited with many wonderful pieces of song and poetry, some of which were published in 1938 as *The Songs of John MacCodrum* and edited by the late William Matheson. MacCodrum was authorised bard to Sir James Macdonald. The occasion

Seal-folk

of his obtaining this situation was as follows:

> He made a satirical piece on all the tailors of the Long Island [OUTER HEBRIDES], at which they were so exasperated that they would not work for him on any account. One consequence of this was, that John soon became a literal tatterdemalion. Sir James meeting him one day, inquired the reason of his being thus clad. John explained. Sir James desired him to repeat the verses – which he did; and the piece was so much to Sir James' liking, that John was forthwith promoted to be his bard, and obtained free lands on his estate in North Uist.

John MacCodrum died in 1779 and his remains are buried in Kilmuir cemetry where a memorial stone erected in 1894 marks his final resting place.

Seal-folk

The MacOdrums of Uist achieved fame across the Atlantic ocean as well; one of them, the Rev. Donald MacOdrum, was one time Moderator of the Presbyterian Church in Canada, and one of his sons, Dr. Maxwell Murdoch MacOdrum, also a Presbyterian clergyman, was to became President of Carleton College (now Carleton University), Ottawa. The alteration to the spelling of the name is cognate with many others which underwent unintentional change through the sundry documentations required by emigration shipmasters and their agents, who may have been quite unfamiliar with the Gaelic language or with contemporary English renderings of those names.

Sometimes known as *Clann 'ic Mhanuis* (the sons of Magnus), *Clann 'ic Odrum nan Ròn* have been identified with the Old Norse name Guðørmr (the good, or god, serpent). A stalwart son of the Hebrides, quite probably the Norse jarl of the same name, is known to have been in command of Hakon's fleet in the year 1263. 'Eyfari ok Guðørmr Suðreyinger, a sinu skipi hvarr.'(from the Hakonar Saga [Rolls Series] 335).

In a lonely glen in North Harris, this name still endures. Lag MacGodrum ('MacGodrum's hollow') identifies the site, along with the ruin of his house, of one MacGodrum who, according to local knowledge, lived there for some considerable time, long before the castle at Amhuinnsuidhe was built in 1868. It is not known for certain where he came from, but he was probably one of the North Uist MacCodrums. He may have been employed by *Fear Huisinis*, the tacksman at Husinish farm, or else for some other obscure reason he chose to live in North Harris. What is important however is the way the name is now spelt 'Godrum', even appearing in this form on modern maps of the area – this rendering of the name exactly follows the Gaelic pronounciation, and is also as close as can be to the Old Norse original..

Seal-folk

Also sharing the same Norse identity, and possibly connected in some way with the MacCodrums, is the place-name 'Odar', which appears in several locations on North Uist. One such site is Caisteal Odair, or 'Odar Castle' – an elevated headland in Griminish which had massive defence works on the landward side of the promontory. Here are to be found the imprints of Odar's heels, where he is said to have landed after vaulting from Ha'sgeir over seven miles away, in order to save his wife from imminent danger. She must have been an even more extraordinary woman to have justified this gigantic endeavour by Odar! There is also an expanse of the sea known as Caolas Od-Odrum, or 'the Kyle of Odrum', which lies to the west of the Monach Isles. The Kyle of Odrum is beautifully described in the poignant lament of the Seal-folk:

>Ann an caolas Od-odrum
>Far an caidleadh an ròn,
>'S far nach cluinnteadh guth duine
>Ach fuaim tuinne 's glog geòidh.
>Mar mhuime 'g altrum a pàisdean
>'S i 'g an tàladh gu ciùin,
>Gu bheil tulgadh nan cuantan
>'G ar sior luasgadh 'n ar suain.
>Tha 'n ròn rioghal ag gùsgail,
>'S an eala 'guileag r'a thaobh,
>'S a' Mhaighdean Mhara 's i 'bruadar
>Anns an uaigneas air laoch.
>'S theid na luingeas a bhathadh,
>'S theid na h- armuinn a dhith,
>'S cha laigh suain air an ainnir
>Gun a leannan sa ' chill.
>Och! an duthaich an eorna
>Cha sguir comhrag no eug,
>'S gum bi dòruinn chloinn-daoine
>Leis an aois dol am meud.
>Ach bidh mise 's mo leannan
>Chaoidh 'n ar flaitheas fo thuinn,
>'S cha ruig airsneal no aois oirnn
>Gus an saorar nan suinn.

Seal-folk

In yon Sound of Odrum,
Where sleepth grey phoca;
Where no voice of mankind is
But of waves and of lag-geese.

As a step-dame her nurslings,
So gently them hushing,
The rocking sea billows
E'r lull us to slumber.

The seal-royal is booming,
The fair swan sings beside him;
On her couch dreams the mermaid
Of her swain on the dry land.

The barks are a-sailing
With their crews through the channels,
Seeking perils so bravely,
For love and music and honour.

And the barks all will be lost,
And their crews all will perish,
And there's no sleep for the maidens,
With their brave ones unburied.

In the land of the barley[UIST]
Will strife and death be unceasing,
And the anguish of mankind
Will with age be increasing.

But I and my heart's love,
In our heav'n 'neath the billows,
Shall be ageless and tireless
Till the brave are released.

Traditional: Translation by Rev. A.M. Macfarlane
(1923)

The late Reverend Archibald MacDonald, who collected much of John MacCodrum's songs and poetry, was obviously quite aware of the MacCodrums' speculative pedigree, but at the same time he was necessarily cautious regarding his own acquiesence to the popular theory. He did, however, agree that the

Seal-folk

unique deference shown by the island people to the seals was due to their large, soft eyes, and the appealing attraction of their semi-human expression.

The Sons of Magnus, from whom the MacCodrum clan reputedly had its origins, did not continue in the recent history of the Hebrides, but they are very well known from oral folklore, and I first learned of their tradition around forty years ago from the lobster-fishermen of Grimsay. The same Sons of Magnus are also mindfully recorded in Professor D.A. Fergusson's inestimable collection, *The Hebridean Connection: Accounts and Stories of the Uist Sennachies*

> In the days of the Lords (of the Isles) the *tairrsearachd* was entrusted to *Clann 'ic Mhanuis*, men who were deemed in those ages to be strong men. The old song was saying: 'The men in whom is *cloidh*, The big men who are in Haisgeir' ...It was said that the children of the son of Odrum were of them and there was in an old song:
>
> *Clann 'ic Odrum nan ròn,*
> *Siol nam fear mòr a bha 'n Haisgeir;*
> *Bho Mhanus, fear ceannsail an sàil,*
> *An armunn a thainig bho Lochlan.*
>
> Children of the son of Odrum of the seals,
> The seed of the big men of Haisgeir,
> From Magnus, conqueror of the brine,
> The hero who came from Lochlan[NORWAY].

Those sons of Magnus had the widest possible authority over all maritime affairs, in their duties as the Ocean Constabulary of the Lords of the Isles. Like a private 'coastguard' service, they were privileged to patrol a vast area of the ocean from their base in the Hebrides in return for whatever the sea provided for them. What appears to have been a particularly strenuous and demanding responsibility in order to gain a perilous existence is evident from the following lines:

Seal-folk

Ceicidh tu an Coire Brùg,
Dol a nùll gu Arcamh,
Freicidh tu an Coire Leathann,
Dol a sin gu Fàra;
Sgealamaid tu na Coirean Aoga,
Smeoslaichidh tu Boireidh,
Cuairtichidh tu Rocabarraidh,
For an laigh am foidhirlisg.

You shall oversee the Coire Brug,
Going over to Orkney:
You shall oversee the wide Coire,
Going from there to Faroe;
You shall oversee the deathly Coire,
You shall oversee Boreray,
You shall circumnavigate Rocabarraidh,
Where lies the *foidhirlisg*[THE SOURCE OF SEA-WARE]

Those Celtic Vikings were the masters of a particular type of longship known as a *scolp*, which transported them safely through the ocean's most fearsome cauldrons – the *Coire Brug* (the erupting cauldron) or the Pentland Firth; the *Coire Leathann* (the expansive cauldron) between the Faroes and Orkney; and the *Coire Aog* (the deathly cauldron) between the Faroes and the Hebrides. They were reputed to have been based on the inhospitable rocks of Ha'sgeir; and it is interesting to note that the nearest landfall about seven miles away on the North Uist coast, at Griminish Point, is a small bay called Scolpaig, the name derived from Scolp-vik in the Old Norse tongue.

Seal-folk

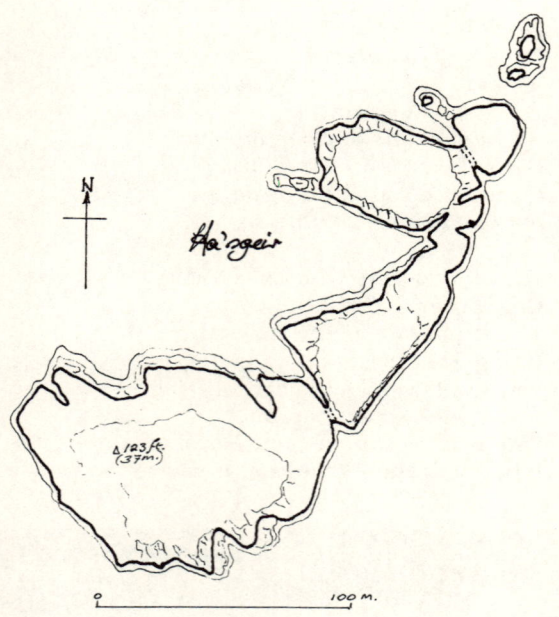

Ha'sgeir, the Ocean Rock, is actually two groups separated by a mile of sea, with the main island which reaches from 80 to 123 feet above sea level having around three to four acres of rich soil supporting a lush maritime vegetation. It sustains a healthy breeding colony of Grey seals, but I would imagine it to be a most precarious location for a human population, apart from brief periods of good weather in summer time.

The late Robert Atkinson, whose love of the pure nature of the Hebrides permeates his writing, describes Ha'sgeir as he first approached it in his converted fishing boat 'Heather':

> Haskeir began as a monotone lump against the light but soon the silhouette resolved into sharp crags, tusks and overhangs; two sea tunnels opened up, cutting clean through the rock like a couple of windows. We got close up to the rock walls and cruised up and down.

Seal-folk

> A few seals slid into the water; the place was alive with the stir of a seabird rock, the circling auks and fulmars, the whitened ledges, the rows of shags flopping down into the water, the rafts of birds floating offshore (*Shillay and the Seals*, p. 50)

Sliochd nan Ròn indeed! To venture thus far on the ocean, and to survive where it does not appear humanly possible, they certainly were 'champions' of the sea. Descended from the seals? Well, I personally believe that folklore should win the day, and moreover, I have a powerful desire to discover, if at all possible, the reality beyond the myth. Surely ancient mariners who were endowed with such impressive aquatic skills and supreme courage deserve our most humble respect, and for them, a permanent place in history.

There is an old Gaelic saying, *An giomach, an rionnach, 's an ròn; tri seòid a chuain*: The lobster, the mackerel, and the seal – the three champions of the ocean: the undisputed masters of their natural environment. Of this aquatic trinity, the Atlantic Grey Seal is champion of champions, and probably not so much simply because of its extraordinary prowess in the water, but on account of its inquisitive and sociable nature, which so endears it to humans, or just maybe, partly because of its supposedly supernatural powers which foster a sense of awe and uncertainty in a naturally superstitious people. In Norwegian maritime traditions, the Grey Seal is 'king of the deep'.

~ 2 ~

CHAMPION OF CHAMPIONS

Atlantic grey,
    grim, foreboding;
beating, pounding, carving, roaring,
    on ancient rocks of time.

Broken shorelines,
    golden grains of sand;
transcendent, Isles of eternal youth,
    and weeping Atlantic Grey.

John Macaulay

It would be extremely egotistical to overlook, or even momentarily to take for granted, the remarkable creatures which share in our mystery of metamorphosis. Whilst it is all too easy to assume that everyone knows what a seal is anyway, and that subsequently no description is necessary, it must be realised that the majority of people have only seen seals either on film or else in the artificial environment of a zoo, or at a marine life centre.

Strangely, the 'Common' Seal is not at all the most common. The more numerous species of seals around the Scottish coast is the Grey Seal, or the Atlantic Grey Seal as it is sometimes known – and it is the Grey Seal that is most often associated with the mystery of metamorphosis. So as to understand a little about this large aquatic mammal, let us for a moment just snatch a glimpse of its secluded life.

The name 'seal' is applied collectively to the marine mammals of the order Pinnipedia, so called from the Latin words meaning wing-footed since the extremities

Champion of Champions

are formed or modified into relatively short but very strong swimming paddles or flippers. There are two quite distinct families within this order: the *Phocidae* – the true seals which have no external ears, and the *Otariidae* – the eared seals or sea-lions. From the eighteen species of true seals, only two of which are relevant to our legends of the seal-folk, we have the Harbour or 'Common' Seal, or *Phoca vitulina*, and the Grey Seal of the Atlantic, *Halichoerus grypus*. Both species are native to approximately the same coastal areas of the British Isles, Scandinavia, Iceland, and Newfoundland.

All seals are generally described as carnivorous mammals adapted to a marine existence. And how splendidly adapted they are too is evident if we examine the exceptional characteristics of their instinctive behaviour. They may well appear to be ungainly and sluggish when hauled out ashore, whether basking on sea-washed rocks or lumbering massively along a sandy beach. Even when seen on the surface of the water they

Champion of Champions

give the impression of thoroughly enjoying an intensely relaxed lifestyle, only diving occasionally for food. Submerged, however, where they enter their own chosen environment, they display the true characteristics of their adaptation to the greatest effect. Here, in the depths of the ocean, they are champion.

Seals can swim underwater much faster than they appear to do on the surface, and can easily attain speeds of nine and a half knots, or eleven miles per hour. Sprint speeds in excess of this are possible when chasing a tasty morsel like the fast swimming mackerel. The duration and depth of their dives are equally astonishing. Harbour (Common) Seals normally submerge for a period of five minutes and slightly longer; and the maximum recorded duration is twenty-eight minutes! Larger seals can remain underwater for proportionately longer periods; so the Grey Seal would therefore be expected to surpass the diving potential of the smaller Harbour Seal. This extraordinary capacity is achieved by the seal's ability to store large amounts of oxygen, not only in its lungs which are proportionately larger than those of a terrestrial mammal, but likewise in a greater volume of blood. In a slowing down of the metabolism, the seal's heart rate, which is normally around fifty to sixty beats per minute on the surface of the water is reduced to as low as ten beats per minute during a long deep dive. On returning to the surface the heart rate can increase dramatically up to one hundred and fifty beats per minute before it gradually settles down again to its normal rate. When diving in shallow water the seal relies mainly on the very large air capacity of its lungs; but for lengthy dives to greater depths it is the physical ability to store reserve oxygen in haemoglobin and in muscle tissues which sustains this remarkable creature. In fact most of the air in the lungs is forcibly expelled before they commence a deep dive, otherwise they would risk introducing nitrogen bubbles into the blood stream

Champion of Champions

when resurfacing. The whole body of the seal and its vital organs automatically compensate for the enormous pressures encountered at depth, counteracting the abnormal effects which can seriously cripple or even prove fatal to a human diver exposed to similar conditions.

The Grey Seal forsakes its maritime environment and comes ashore during the breeding season, which in the Scottish west coast islands begins in the month of September. Large colonies assemble on the traditional breeding grounds of the offshore islets well away from human habitation. Robert Atkinson was the first to study the habits of the Grey Seals during this short period of frantic activity, on the island of Shillay, the most westerly of the Sound of Harris group of islands.

Shillay is within sight of a number of other Grey Seal colonies, which are included in Atkinson's description of the view from the seventy-seven metre grassy summit – Gasker and Haskeir, which along with Shillay comprised at that time 'the three main seal nurseries of the Atlantic coast'. The seals haul out on conveniently sheltered beaches and many of them head inland for some considerable distance, competing for space with the ubiquitous sheep innocuously grazing on grassy hillsides. On the lower ground soft marshy hollows quickly degenerate into extensive mud baths, especially when ferociously churned by frenzied bulls competing for supremacy. Pups usually arrive in the first hour of dawn with a beautifully white coat which lasts only for the three weeks of lactation, after which they moult, and then they acquire the characteristic colouring of the parent during the next week or two prior to their entering the sea for the first time. The Grey Seal pup trebles its body weight during this time of feeding from its mother, who does not return to the sea to feed herself until after her offspring is weaned. The mothers' eventual return to the water is not without incident. The bull seals bar their progress, and mating has to take

Champion of Champions

place before this annual cycle of reproduction is complete. Blatant promiscuity seems too refined a term to describe the frenetic activity on the crowded beach, and in the breaking surf, which turns red with blood as the salacious orgy to procure next year's brood continues relentlessly. No holds are barred, and the younger bulls will bear the scars for the rest of their years. Eventually, however, peace prevails and all return to the sea; and the pups which were born on Shillay will disperse and maybe venture even as far as the Bay of Biscay before returning as young adults to re-enact the drama of Hebridean proliferation. The rarely seen cute and cuddly seal pups all too quickly take on the familiar form and extraordinary characteristics which identify them as champions.

It is little wonder, then, that our fascination with those creatures extends to a mythological association. From the earliest of times, man's desire to master the ocean would produce an envy and a powerful desire to emulate the superior aquatic ability of the seal. Even to reach out in a spiritual sense, and to convey our rudimentary desire in poetic fantasy, is maybe to express our gratification in sharing at least a partial fulfilment of those aspirations through our primitive relationship with a remarkably endearing mammal.

~ 3 ~

HEBRIDEAN AND NORSE TRADITION

And in the light the white mermaiden swam,
And strong man-breasted things stood from the sea,
And sent a deep sea voice through all the land.

Alfred Lord Tennyson, *Idylls of the King*.

There is a striking similarity between Norwegian folklore – especially from the Northern coast and islands – and Hebridean oral tradition. Alasdair Alpin Macgregor in *The Peat Fire Flame* states:

> Scandinavian Folklore is rich in allusion to a curious race inhabiting the archipelagoes, and known as the Finn-folk. These elusive creatures are akin, it is said, to the users of kayaks. They are described like the Esquimos, as spending most of their lives in paddling through the narrow fjords in light canoes covered over with seal-skin. During the 17th century, and probably at a date more recent, Orcadian waters were occasionally visited by Finns, who paddled in and about them in kayaks. This is borne out by contemporary writers.

The archipelagoes mentioned are those of Lofoten and Vesterålen, which according to *Heimskringla* xiv, are known to have been inhabited by the 'Finns' around one thousand years ago. These Finns have been known by various names, but mostly they are referred to as Skrijkfinnar or Skraelings.

It is most important to bear in mind, first of all, the question of exactly who those people were who settled in the Outer Hebrides for a period of around five

Hebridean and Norse Tradition

Hebridean and Norse Tradition

hundred years. It is all too easy to accept the universal concept of being invaded by marauding hordes of Vikings, with their reputation for perpetrating all kinds of nasty deeds almost as a form of bloodthirsty entertainment, as being that particular people who imposed themselves on the island populations and reigned superior for half a millenium. But that was not just exactly as it happened!

Unfortunately, apart from obscure evidence of rudimentary settlements and several perplexing archaeological features, there is not a great deal known about Hebridean history prior to the Norse settlement. Johannes Brønsted, in *The Vikings*, makes an interesting suggestion regarding the existing inhabitants which the Norsemen 'joined or replaced' in stating 'There is archaeological evidence for the belief that, when the Viking raids began, these islands (Shetland, Orkney, Hebrides) were already, to some extent, occupied by Norwegians who had found them virtually uninhabited.'

However, in 794 A.D. the Vikings began their devastation of the British Isles; and from that time on, for around eighty years, the Norðreyjar, or the Northern Isles of Orkney and Shetland; and the Suðreyjar, or the Southern Isles, the Inner and Outer Hebrides including the Isle of Man, were occupied by independent Vikings. Then in the second half of the ninth century, Harald Haarfagr (Fairhair) King of Norway, overthrew the Viking regime in the Scottish Islands to accommodate people who were forcibly displaced from their own lands in the north-west regions of Norway – from Møre northwards, including the Vesterålen and Lofoten islands.

Those *Lochlannaich*, Norwegians, who were to settle in the islands from Shetland to the Isle of Man, spreading also to Faroe and Iceland, eventually to colonise Greenland and even to reach North America, were quite different people to the Danes (Southern Norway, Sweden and Denmark), who colonised the east

Hebridean and Norse Tradition

coast of Scotland, England and also the European countries from the Baltic to the Mediterranean Sea. The people of the North were from an entirely different culture and society; and the unique imprint of their origin is, to this day, very evident in the native Hebridean.

> The native Islesmen, particularly from certain areas, still bear a strong resemblance to the people of Norway; and not only in physical appearance, but also in their remarkable ability to survive, and exist in harmony with, an extremely harsh environment. The most outstanding quality the islanders have inherited, though, is their skill on the ocean. Sailors and fishermen throughout the ages have wrought a living from the sea, learning from an early age masterful proficiency in seamanship, and daring – tempered with respect.
>
> John Macaulay, *Birlinn*

The Rev. Macfarlane also, in an address to the Inverness Scientific Society (1923) acknowledged this hereditary trait in the native Hebridean:

> The Hebridean Celt always in sight and sound of the sea, cannot help being influenced thereby. Nevertheless he can when the occasion demands overcome the awe, the dread that the unfriendly elements helped to inspire.
>
> In proof of that where will you find more intrepid seamen than among the Hebrideans from Barra Head to the Butt of Lewis? It is a well-known fact that instead of cravenly yielding to fear when in a storm, their spirits rise with the danger, and so does their coolness. Feeling and imagination for the time being are kept under control.There seems to be a hidden mettle in them evoked to cope with the menace of the moment.They have evinced the same indomitable and healthy spirit of battling in war.
>
> What is it due to? (for is it not in all the Celtic peoples?) Nothing can account for it but the strain of

Hebridean and Norse Tradition

the Norse-race in their blood. It has been observed in Hebridean sailors that at critical moments in a storm at sea the lustiness of their songs has successfully vied with that of the wind. Not only so, but that they have indulged in peals of Homeric laughter. It is exactly the same over-seeing sense of superior power that has made the Berserk.

You would expect that this combination of two distinct cultures, from differing ethnic backgrounds, but commonly moulded by a like geography and maritime environment, would result in the establishment of a unique society; yet following the return of the Islands to the Scottish crown, there appears to have been a rapid reversion to the Celtic identity and way of life. I say, there *appears* to have been, for I strongly believe that deeply rooted in all native Islanders is a far greater measure of Norse blood than there is of Celt. Even the language which we tend to accept as unquestionably pure *Gaidhlig*, has absorbed far more of the Old Norse tongue than is commonly realised; and part of our language which we use daily, is just exactly as the Norse people used it. It is well known that in Shetland the 'Norrn' dialect evolved from Old Norse, and even into the early part of the eighteenth century it was the only language known in some places: John Brand, who, in the year 1700, visited Shetland and Orkney on behalf of the General Assembly of the Church of Scotland, states that there were 'Some who spoke none other than Norfe in the parish of Hara'

The reality of the Norse occupation is still very much in evidence; the principal place-names of the Hebrides instantly betray their source, and all of them, endowed with an illustrative terminology, demonstrate the use of language as an effective means of navigation – a system still in use by some of the older inshore fishermen. From Norway I would have expected to find much more evidence concerning this part of their

Hebridean and Norse Tradition

national history, but sadly, that is not the case. The old language itself no longer exists as such, since it was superseded by Danish, to which the modern Norwegian language is very close. In fact Iceland was the last stronghold of the Old Norse tongue, both written and spoken, as is known from the evidence of the sagas, which were mainly written around the thirteenth century.

The ease with which Britt Sneltvedt accepted my description of the apparently inhospitable oceanic rocks west of the Hebrides as a suitable location for the existence of 'Seal-folk', once again demonstrates how an alien people can establish themselves, and for some considerable time (the Norse occupation was for a period of around five hundred years), and then fade away with hardly a trace of their ever having been. The reality behind the traditions of the Seal-folk in the Hebrides is now concealed in folklore, in the legend of the MacCodrums, and of several other families who share this unique pedigree.

According to Britt, the equivalent of our Seal-folk in Norway, who are the Sjø-Sami people (that is, the coastal Lapps who inhabited the offshore islands) were never highly esteemed by the Norwegian people. They were in fact considered to be of the lowest social order; described as 'generally very ignorant, simple-hearted, and hospitable'; and it is only in very recent times that any interest has been expressed, and serious enquiry made, both politically and historically, into their culture and traditions.

It would be somewhat capricious of me to describe those people whose history of settlement is as far-reaching and infinitely varied as the nomadic lifestyle of their ancestors. Nevertheless, a brief look into their origin and present status may be helpful, if only to establish in our mind their identity within a circumpolar society. Today, even though the Sami people are

Hebridean and Norse Tradition

accepted as citizens of Norway, they are still described as 'an ethnic minority and a separate people'. However, they are now recognised as being worthy of the respect of the *Storting* – the Norwegian Government – and in 1987 an Act concerning the status of the Sami, forming the mechanism for a national assembly, was approved by the *Storting*. This long overdue change in attitude led to the establishment of the Sami Parliament, the *Sameting*, which for the first time in their history gives the Sami people rights and control over their own affairs. It was officially opened on the 9th of October 1989 by the late King Olav V.

So it can be seen that it is only quite recently – in fact only within the last twenty years or so – that this indigenous people, who had inhabited the Nordic regions since at least the beginning of the first millennium, and more than likely for several millennia before, have been dignified with official status and the proper responsibility for managing their own affairs. Their distant cousins the Eskimos, who are known to have inhabited the Arctic regions of the New World, from the Aleutian Islands west of Alaska, across northern Canada to Baffin Island and Greenland, for around four thousand years, were never subjected to any form of servitude such as the Sami were to the 'superior' social classes to the south of them; but the Eskimos also in recent times have suffered from the world's obsessive intent to 'civilise' them. The Sami may have occupied their own Arctic territories for at least the same length of time, but little is known about their early history. What is known is conveniently summarised by Elena Helander:

> The oldest written source of knowledge on the Sami is the Roman historian Tacitus' descriptions of a people whom he called 'Fenni', in the book *De origine et situ Germanorum* written in 98 A.D. In 555 A.D. the Greek historian, Procopius, describes a war waged between

Hebridean and Norse Tradition

the Romans and the Goths. He refers to Scandinavia as 'Thule', and among its inhabitants was a people he referred to as 'skridfinns'. Paulus Diaconus, writing around 750, also mentions the 'skridfinns', describing them as hunters and skiers who kept animals resembling deer (reindeer). The Icelandic sagas confirm these observations. Written largely in the 13th century, the sagas cover a period from about the tenth to the thirteenth century A.D.

The Sami traditionally were hunters and trappers based in small comunities known as siidas; the prolific fishing and rich hunting in this northern area providing food, fur, and ivory. In the seventeenth century the sparsely populated extensive coastal and inland region from Nordland to Finmark was the territory chosen to be colonised by farmers – 'a source of livelihood which contrasted strongly with the traditional Sami occupations.' Existing survival skills were adapted to suit their new environment, and were developed with subsequent generations to reach that finely honed edge where man and nature meet.

Broadly described as one of four branches of the Ural-Altaic division of the Turanian family of peoples and languages, their physiognomy is characterised by low stature, though of strong muscular build; low forehead, and features which are flat with prominent cheekbones and oblique eyes.

Nelson Annandale, in the early years of this century, was to record this Mongoloid semblance in Icelandic and Faroese people: 'It is a historic fact', he says, 'that in the ninth century and earlier the Scandinavians intermarried with the Lapps or 'Finns', as they were called. ...Moreover', continues Mr. Annandale, 'Beddoe, than whom we could have no safer guide in physical anthropology, believes that physical traces of Mongolian ancestry can be detected in the Shetlanders'.

A relatively unknown and little understood people, nevertheless they made their mark in the most

Hebridean and Norse Tradition

unexpected manner. Harald Haarfagr, the King of Norway from 863 – 933, was to marry one of them! She was Snaefrid, the daughter of Svase the Finn, or Lapp. Three of their sons became Norwegian jarls, and a fourth, Halfdan Haaleg, held the lordship of Orkney for a whole summer. And we need not be greatly surprised to learn that it was the same King Harald who conquered the whole of the Hebrides, and repopulated those islands with his own subjects whom he forcibly evicted from the west coast and north of Norway.

Why, then, should we still question the evidence of their presence in the Scottish Islands? Why should native folklore be doubted, or even relegated to the realm of fantasy? The very existence of 'Seal-folk', who could have come from no other place than Norway, is as certain as is the evidence of those families whom we know of, who are the progeny of *na Lochlannaich*.

Various accounts of their presence in Scottish waters have been recorded over the years, and most of those point to a Norse origin, as in the following examples:

> *Finn-folk*, the name given in Orkney to a sea-faring race who occasionally visited these isles during the latter part of the 17th century. Their canoes were exactly similar to the *kayaks* of the Eskimos. Shetland tradition refers to a race of 'Finns' who came across from Norway, and whose attributes are those of the 'Finn-folk' of Orkney folklore. Orkney tradition speaks of the Finn as the aborigines of the group. As 'Finn' is the Norse for 'Lapp', and as the Orkney and Shetland people are radically Norse, it would seem that these Finns were really 'Lapps' and Von Duben mentions that existing Lapps speak of the little skin canoes of their ancestors.
>
> *Nelson's Encyclopaedia*

Captain Frederick W.L. Thomas, writing in the 1860s, suggested an early movement of a primitive people throughout all the coastal regions as the ice

Hebridean and Norse Tradition

receded. We must also bear in mind that significant climatic changes took place during the second half of the seventeenth century, when it got much colder and ice cover once again extended considerably further south than at present. On the topography of the Hebrides Capt. Thomas remarked:

> All these phenomena are due to ice, and subsequent water ....Without entering further on that subject, I may remark that the sharpness of the glacial phenomena in the Hebrides conveys to the observer that the close of the ice period is not so far distant. Whenever it occurred, colonies of men would no doubt follow up the coasts in the same manner in which the Esquimaux have distributed themselves in the Arctic regions. As the climate ameliorated, vegetation would increase, and a littoral mode of life – apparently the most primitive of all – would be mixed up with and partly superceded, by a pastoral one. I do not believe that the hunter state could have had any long continuance in the limited area of Britain. Now, the primitive people of our island and of the whole of Europe were most probably of the Turanian division, and are represented in Europe by the Laps and Fins; nor do I doubt that, in the short faces of some of the Connaught boys, we have very near copies of the good-natured physiognomy of our earliest immigrants. An accomplished writer, [Lord Dufferin's *Letters from High Latitudes*, p. 254] having no ethnological fancies in his head, is struck by the resemblance of a Lapland family to some of the Irish, where he says 'there was a merry, half-timid, half-cunning twinkle in their eyes, which reminded me a little of the faces I had met with in the more neglected parts of Ireland.' My own opinion is that this race held possession for thousands of years; that they developed with the improvement of the climate; and that to them we owe the remarkable stone monuments existing here. For the history of the succeeding Keltic race is partially known for 2000 years, yet no notice is to be found, that

Hebridean and Norse Tradition

I am aware of, that they ever erected a stone circle; indeed, the inference is plainly in the opposite direction.

Proc. Soc. Antiq. Scot., V11: pp 193/4 (1867)

Adding to the problem surrounding the identity of strangers to our shores, though in another sense it may be a reflection of the same tradition, is the identity of the legendary *Fian* of Celtic tradition. So who were the *Fian,* or *Feinne* (Fingalians)? This somewhat obscure branch of Celtic lore received much attention from scholars in the early part of this century. Without entering too deeply into it now, a peep into the past will be sufficient to place them in context, and to note some of the similarities with the Finns or Lapps.

Existing in the Gaelic tradition of Ireland and Scotland as a great warrior caste, there are many marvellous tales of their courageous exploits and magnificent triumphs of good over evil. There had for long been a notion that the *Feinne* 'were a body of Irish militia, forming a kind of standing army, employed for the purpose of defending the coasts of Ireland from the invasion of foreign foes;' and moreover, according to Keating, 'when looked at a little more closely, they ... assume the features of a distinct race'. This race he believed to have been the precursors of the Gaels in Ireland and Scotland, and of the Germanic races in 'Lochlan'.

Does this not accord with the description by Tacitus of the 'fenni' in Scandinavia; and the 'Fenner' of whom the great Ghengis Khan once said he would never fight with them again? Dr. Skene thought that the *Feinne* are identified with the Picts – the precursors of the Gaels – occupying underground dwellings and mound structures; the remains of which are found throughout Scotland and its Islands. Indeed the diversity of archaeological remains in their various locations throughout the Islands are as much of a mystery in themselves, as are the people who built and occupied them

Hebridean and Norse Tradition

It is notoriously difficult to identify a single common denominator in such an extensive sphere of folklore on which to rest a thesis, and indeed that is not the purpose of this study; but rather it is the intent to present as broad a picture as possible, drawing on varied sources both written and oral. Nevertheless, there is a recurring theme even now in briefly examining the legend of the *Feinne* – as we find in a tale of Fin's voyage in his skin boat to the 'Kingdom of the Big Men' where he became a court dwarf! There is nearly always this contrast in physical stature, with the hero of the story portrayed as the 'ordinary' type whether confronted by dwarf or by giant.

In this story Fin was lifted up by the King in the palm of his hand! Then there is the association with supernatural powers – a handful of pebbles became a house, and a bunch of wood shavings became the furnishings, and we meet a soothsayer. There is also the boat, albeit described as a

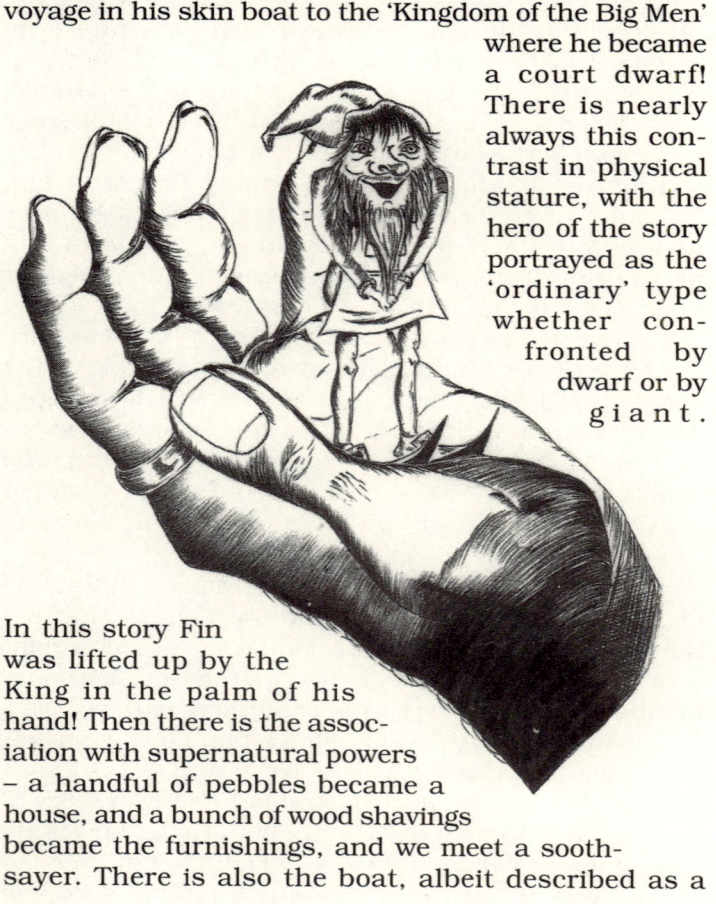

Hebridean and Norse Tradition

coracle, although one would expect a *curragh* coming from Ireland.

The details are increasingly shrouded by the passing of the years; but yet we have this distinct picture of a small person in a skin boat.

One of the principal attributes recognised as being commonly shared by the Seal-folk of the Hebrides, the Finn-folk of Shetland and Orkney, and the Lapps of Northern Norway is their supposed ability to harness supernatural powers. The folklorist Guerber described the Lapps thus: 'This people who lived in the frozen regions of the pole, besides being able to call up the cold storms which swept down from the North, bringing much ice and snow in their train, were supposed to have great occult powers.'

The Seal-folk, already endowed with extraordinary maritime skills, were nearly always attributed with supernatural powers, which alone would be sufficient to set them apart from ordinary people. Able to predict and to control the weather; practising magic, soothsaying, and sorcery; they also had the power of healing both man and beast.

The *Margygr* or Mermaid, and the *Marmennill* or Merman, with their children who are called *Marmaeler* all have extraordinary powers, according to Kauffman: the children were sometimes caught by the fishermen 'that they may gain from them a knowledge of future events; for both they, as well as the Mermen and Mermaids, can see into futurity.' Another folklorist, Dr. Karl Blind, once wrote, 'they are held to be deeply versed in magic spells and in the healing art, as well as in soothsaying'. And quite remarkable as some of those diverse talents may be, probably the most intriguing of all is that they had the uncanny ability to communicate readily with one another over long distances – through the medium of telepathy. This gift of telepathic transmission was upheld in an article published by

Hebridean and Norse Tradition

Robert Crottet in 1947, entitled *Children of the Wild;* in it we read:

> Beyond the Polar Circle, in the heart of forlorn Finnish Lappland, lives a small tribe, the Scolt Lapps......Unlike so many of the primitive races, they have firmly rejected all efforts to bring them the comforts of our civilisation. They will not have even radio sets in their huts. The noise that comes from a box, they say, spoils the voice of the trees and the never-ending melody of the virgin forest. No wonder if Nature, in return for their faithfulness, has preserved in them the powers we generally call 'second sight'. Telepathy among them is a commonplace; it even enables them to make appointments with one another when they are miles apart. They dream of a place and time, and meet as easily as if they had arranged it by telephone.
>
> A Scolt Lapp will look at you with his clear transparent eyes ... and he will see your real face, your 'second face 'behind the mask ... At times it makes him sad, looking into other people's eyes, to find something like a drooping flower in them, slowly fading from lack of care and proper watering.
>
> ...We need to know that on the confines of Europe are some people who preserve those precious powers we have had to lose in our constant endeavour to master Nature, and sometimes even its Creator.

Crottet recognised in the Scolt Lapps, or the Eastern Sami, something far beyond our indistinct concept of the supernatural; he realised that here were people who lived truly in harmony with nature. They were healthy and happy in a way of life which had already, in 1947, been almost utterly extinguished by civilisation in other cultures, so much so that life for them was a 'perpetual enchantment'. But it is the extraordinary development of the natural senses which set them apart from other people. Even telepathic communication seems mundane in the light of their uncanny ability to enter into and read the mind of others just as a matter of course.

Hebridean and Norse Tradition

It is as if they are able to penetrate the very soul of their fellow beings – phenomenal, but entirely necessary, to be so perfectly intimate with the whole of Creation.

David MacRitchie said of Orkney and Shetland that 'The Finn women are chiefly remembered as witches and fortune-tellers ...They were also skilful in curing disease in men and cattle'. He also recounts that Ranulph Higden wrote – 'that the witches in the Isle of Man anciently sold winds to mariners, and delivered them in knots, tied upon a thread, *exactly as the Laplanders did*'. Most Scottish fishing ports have their own anecdote about women of questionable disposition who sold favourable winds to sailors, in the same manner of knots tied on a thread, well into the beginning of this century; I well remember reports of such women in the Hebridean fishing port of Stornoway – unfortunately, they had in time to give way to steam power, and the science of meteorology!

It appears that this association with magic or sorcery applied to the Grey Seals as well as to humans. In *The Hebridean Connection*, Fergusson has this to say in a note appended to the song *Clann Domhnuil 'ic a' Ròin*:

> In the olden time people had to be observant regarding the way of life of the living things which they came across in day-to-day living and it was said that they believed that one seal kept watch when the rest of the colony were hunting fish to warn in the event of approaching danger. Therefore it was the '*ròn teilich*' [from the first verse] which the people of old termed this seal because it issued '*teil*' that is telephonic messages warning other seals of approaching danger by means of an inbuilt telephonic system. It could be that the observant men of the olden times were correct; it is recorded that the people heard seals in communication with each other – among them Mrs. Marjory Kennedy Fraser. The Greek word 'tele' [at a distance] and the Gaelic words '*teil*' and '*teilid*' are cognate in origin; '*teilid na Sgoil Dhuibh*' indicated the extra-sensory telephonic communications of the system which goes by the name 'black art' in the English language.

Hebridean and Norse Tradition

This connection with the *Sgoil Dhubh* or 'black art' implies the use of extraordinary power, or to put it simply, another 'sense'; which we appear to have lost the use of in our ordinary everyday interaction with our fellow beings. That such an ability was recognised of old in the seals, and even transmitted to certain humans, appears to be supernatural; but after all, are we ourselves not familiar with similar experiences through affinity with domestic animals and pets?

Then there is the story of 'the Ship-master of Aarhuus and the Finlap', which serves to demonstrate (and I'll say this with due caution) imaginatively, the ability to exercise, for whatever intent, the remarkable powers attributed to these people.

> A shipmaster from Aarhuus was once lying at Drontheim [TRONDHEIM], where he formed an acquaintance with a Finlap, who often came on board to visit him. This Finlap, who could perform many sorceries, offered, among other things, to teach the shipmaster how to procure a wind. This, thought the skipper, might be very convenient, and the next day the Finlap brought a bag with him, which he placed outside the cabin, saying, that he needed only to take that with him, and he could make any wind. But the shipmaster on reflection would have no concern with it, suspecting that it came from the devil. The Finlap then asked him whether he wished to know how his wife and children were. On the skipper answering in the affirmative, The Finlap immediately fell down on the deck as if dead. After some time he rose, saying: 'I have been to Aarhuus. Thy wife was sitting drinking coffee; the others were also in good health, though one of the children had been ill. That thou mayest believe my words, – dost thou know this?' at the same time handing him a silver spoon. 'This', said the other, 'thou hast taken from my house in Aarhuus.' And so saying took the spoon and kept it.
>
> After they had been lying some time at Drontheim, the Finlap one morning said: 'Tomorrow we shall be under sail, and shall have a good wind, although you are going southward and I northward. And I will further

Hebridean and Norse Tradition

prove to you that you will not go to Christiania fiord, to purchase a lading, as you think; but will get a better freight than you expect.' On the following morning both were under sail, and the wind changed so that the Jutlander had a fair wind for twelve hours, and afterwards the Fin for twelve hours. When off the isles of Öster-riis the wind for the Jutlander was directly adverse, so that after having beaten about for nights and days, he was at last obliged to seek a port in the Öster-riis islands. There one merchant outbid another in their offers of freight, but being eastward bound for a cargo, he declined their proposals, until a merchant at length offered him a freight to the Issefiord which almost equalled the value of a whole lading. This he could not withstand, but wrote to his owners, that for weighty considerations he had not followed their orders, an announcement which among the parties interested in Aarhuus excited the suspicion that he had lost his wits. On his arrival home after the trip, and when just stepping on shore, being questioned about his freight, he answered: 'I have it in my fob.' This proved highly satisfactory. On coming home to his wife, he inquired: 'How are all here?' – 'Well', was the answer. – 'Has any one been ill?'- 'Yes the young one.' – 'Have you lost anything?' – 'No – yes – no.' – 'Think again.' – 'Yes, a silver spoon.' – 'There it is,' said the skipper, laying it on the table.

F. Kauffman, *Northern Mythology*,
transl. Benjamin Thorpe (1851)

~ 4 ~

MYTHOLOGY, FANTASY

Such previous landings of mermaids as have left a record, have all a flavour of doubt. Even the very circumstantial account of the Bruges sea lady, who was so clever at fancy work, gives occasion to the sceptic. I must confess that I was absolutely incredulous of such things until a year ago. But now, face to face with indisputable facts in my own immediate neighbourhood, and ...

So begins the delightful tale of *The Sea Lady* by H.G. Wells, inspired no doubt by the many legendary accounts of mermaids and other sea creatures of the submarine world which continue to haunt us with an irresistible attraction, and with maybe a secret yearning to peep into the realm of the unknown.

There are those among us who refuse to accept, or are as yet sceptical about any connection between myth and reality. Alfred Gordon Bennett, from a mid-twentieth century standpoint, stated that the mermaid legend runs 'counter to scientific possibility', and also that 'there are understandable and excusable grounds for ignorant and superstitious people believing in them'. John Brand, on the other hand, two and a half centuries previously, had due respect for the credibility of folklore and the status of rational observers:

> Some few things indeed feem Fabulous, nor do I fay they are true, but that they are confidently reported and held to be true by feverals in the Countrey, and being fo remarkable in themfelves, could not well pafs them without fome Observ[n]

I am not sure where this places me. I am certainly not superstitious, at least not in any conscious sense,

Mythology, Fantasy

and if I have been ignorant it is only because I did not have the whole story to begin with. Like John Brand, I now have some reports to hand, and indeed I cannot 'paſs them without ſome Obſerv^n'.

It is extremely difficult, impossible in some instances, to say with any degree of authority what establishes a particular story as being myth, fable, or legend; or where within those fabulous narratives there is an element of fact. Folklore in its true sense is the science of tradition, and the *Handbook of Folklore* defines it thus: 'the comparisons and the identification of the survivals of archaic beliefs, customs, and traditions in modern ages'. Tradition embraces all of the foregoing, and I prefer to place the mystery of the Seal-folk within this wider setting of tradition, recognising at the same time that not all available accounts are verifiable.

Maritime folklore elevates the seal to the status of human beings, even to the extent of attributing a line of royal descent from the Kings of Norway! The Rev. Macfarlane, in a paper he read to the Inverness Scientific Society put it this way:

> The beginning was thus – A certain King of Norway had a family of sons and daughters, all of whom were of incomparable beauty; so greatly so, indeed, as to excite the jealousy of their stepmother, who, learning magic for the purpose, put them under a spell that they would

be neither fish nor animal forever: when on land their desire would be to the sea, and vice-versa when on the sea. That, moreover, they would appear in their original state three times a year at the full moon, so that they might lament their loss at viewing their heritage possessed by aliens; and 'twas said that, were you to see any of them at such periods of manifestation, you could not escape giving your heart's love (like any woman beholding Diarmid's beauty-spot) to him or her as the case might be. The belief may at this time be regarded as childish, but it is not so long ago that such loves and unions between seals and humans were believed to have actually taken place on more than one occasion in the Isles. Indeed, there were septs that went by the cognomen of *'Sliochd nan ròn'*- the race of the seals – one representative family being no less than that of the famous Macodrums, hereditary bards and historians to the great family of Clan-Ranald. Indeed, any one distinguished by high poetic and musical gifts was held to be of *'Sliochd nan ròn'*, and physically they were noted by that warm, dark, liquid kind of eye, that draws by its pathos. Of course it is a well known fact that music has an extraordinary attraction for seals. They will follow a boat for miles where music is being played or even sung; nay, they have been known to come ashore and even enter houses after the same charm. In some of the isles it was not considered lucky to kill them. To show this there is the story of a crew of Canna men who were out once bird shooting, when one of them was so maladroit as to shoot a young seal that he saw floundering in the ebb. But if he did! All of a sudden the sea rose mountains high, and buffeted the boat like an egg-shell in a tossed pail of water. Like the mariners of Tarshish of old, the men concluded some one of them must be pursued by the fairies, and so cast lots to see which was the Jonah. Said one zealot, 'I felt from the outset some misfortune would be sure to befall us for taking two Protestants with us.' Of course this meant that the unfortunate two would have to be devoted to the propitiation of the protector of seals – the sea. But they, thinking more of life than of creed, were ready to forswear the latter, and offered there and

Mythology, Fantasy

then to do so, and the aforesaid zealots, in the absence of a priest, sprinkling a little of the elements on them, forthwith declared them true sons of Holy Mother Church. But still and on the sea raged without the least abatement. It was then that another sage quietly said – 'It appears to me that what we are so terribly suffering for is the blunder of killing the innocent child of *ròn rioghal*' [seal royal]. What we must do – indeed, there is nothing else left us – is to make a vow of repentance never to molest, or allow to be molested again, any of the royal race.' This was heartily acquiesced in by all on board; and no sooner was it done than the sea, as if by magic, became calm, and that night they slept in their own beds instead of, as they at one time fully expected, in the briny.

This, or similar versions, is the oft-related origin of the champion of champions. That is how I heard it, so many times, and remarkably I did not ever doubt it – because the MacCodrums are very real people.

One of my favourite stories from the Hebrides is that of *Bodach Rocabarraigh,* the Old Man of Rockall, a story I heard for the first time on Heisgeir at the fireside in the old schoolhouse which was being used as a bothy by the fishermen during the summer season. I have since had the pleasure of reading the same story countless times in the late Padruig Moireasdan's book *Ugam agus Bhuam.* Padruig was one of the greatest story-tellers of recent times, especially in connection with the ocean and its islands of which he was so fond. He had returned with his young family to Heisgeir just after the second world war, in the fervent hope that others would follow them, and once again repopulate this group of fertile oceanic islands. After four years of solitude they left and settled on Grimsay, leaving their beloved islands to adjust once again to nature. Heisgeir, or the Monach Isles as they have been called, at one time supported a religious establishment, referred to in 1549 by Dean Munro as 'Helsker na Caillach pertaining to the Nunnis of Colmkill.' This beautiful and historically

Mythology, Fantasy

fascinating group of small islands remain uninhabited, like many of the oceanic outliers of the Hebrides: home now to teeming seabirds, colonies of Grey Seals, and distant memories of a one time flourishing and healthy population.

Padruig's particular style of story-telling loses much of its character in translation. His was the traditional *ceilidh* style, relaxed, unhurried, and quite distinctive in that every story was told as if for the very first time; and since it is inevitable that the written word must detract from this peculiar quality, I apologise for not being able to convey that same intensity of spirit.

The story of *Bodach Rocabarraidh* is from generations past, and in the times when the west coast of Uist extended much further beyond its present shoreline. A substantial amount of the land was lost, according to oral tradition, during a period of severe storms and an earthquake, which included the machair island of Flodaidh, immediately west of Heisgeir. The Exchequer Rolls, Vol. xvii, p 557, reports a reduction in North Uist rentals in 1542 due to 'encroachment of the sea'. The machair coast continues to be eroded by the sea at a considerable rate.

Anyway, as the story goes, a young man came ashore on the west coast of Uist saying he had been lost in a thick fog for many days, and could not find his way back to where he came from. He stayed from that time in Uist and made his living from the sea, eventually marrying and raising a family of three sons and one daughter. His sons also, following in their father's footsteps, had chosen to devote their lives to fishing. At a time when fish was scarce, and the boys had to venture further out in the ocean, they happened to catch one day some fish which they had not seen before. When they returned and told their father, he asked them to take him with them on their next fishing trip. They did so, and after spending some time in thick fog they arrived at an island further to the west than they had

Mythology, Fantasy

ever been before – and this was where their father had left from so many years ago. He persuaded his sons to leave him behind, and they themselves returned to their home on Uist.

This legend of *Bodach Rocabarraidh* ties in neatly with many other tales in the traditions which perceive Rockall as being the last remaining part of the long-lost continent of Atlantis. Was there indeed some massive catastrophic event which caused an immense area of land to be swallowed up in the ocean? Does the St. Kildan apocalyptic expression relate to this lost landscape reappearing once more? Why have we not heard any more about the 'Uist' family of B*odach Rocabarraidh?* Was the *Bodach* one of the 'Seal-folk'?

Rockall today enjoys a worldwide reputation since its occupation by Greenpeace in the summer of 1997, as part of their protest against oil exploration in the North Atlantic. Positioned at Latitude 57°36'41" N. and Longitude 13°41'25" W, '... the stack of Rockall, some one hundred and eighty miles west of St. Kilda, rises from near the verge of the submerged platform on which the British Islands rest. A few miles west of it the sounding line goes down abruptly, from one hundred to two hundred fathoms, and thereafter with swift descent down to the abysmal depths of the Atlantic'. That is how Erskine Beveridge described this isolated rock. In another description of the rock James A. Mackintosh warns that this is 'Scotland's most dangerous rock ... The most isolated speck of Rock, surrounded by water, on the surface of the earth'. The rich fishing grounds in the area of Rockall were well known to the intrepid fishermen of Heisgeir, who regularly sailed the two hundred-odd miles into the Atlantic to hunt for basking sharks and whales. This sea area was also known to be under the jurisdiction of the Sons of Magnus, the legendary *tairrsearain-fairge*. The name *Rocsail* is the one which was more familiar to the Hebridean fishermen, a literal translation being

Mythology, Fantasy

Sea-rock; this could well be the source of the English version 'Rockall'. Martin Martin describes it thus: 'Rokol, a small rock sixty leagues to the westward of St. Kilda; the inhabitants of this place call it Rokabarra'. Indeed, the St Kildans had rather more to say, in the way of a disturbing warning – *Nuair a thig Rocabarra ris, is dual gun teid an Saoghal a sgrios*: 'If Rocabarra rises, it's inevitable the world will be destroyed'!

Padruig's *Bodach Rocabarraidh* always reminded me of one of the greatest mysteries of my younger years – the *duine mara*. I can yet feel the chill in my spine, and in later years, the trepidation of navigating a particular stretch of water entirely on my own during the hours of darkness on a very wet and windy night.

I first heard of the *duine mara*, or merman, as a young lad in Harris. Every summer season the sheltered bay below our house became a temporary home to visiting lobster boats from the neighbouring Isle of Scalpay. It was our duty, that is, my brother's and mine, to fulfil the hospitality normally extended to any visitors. Fresh milk, butter from the churn, crowdie, scones and oatcakes, were ferried out daily in our little rowing boat, in exchange only for the privilege of being allowed on board to share a mug of tea in the warmth of the fo'c'sle, and for a short moment to feel as if we were part of the crew.

It is interesting now to recall the basic items of equipment they had in those boats, compared with the electronic gadgetry of modern fishing vessels. A family bible – Gaelic of course – and neatly covered with several layers of brown wrapping paper, with an outer layer of oilskin (most likely from the back panel of an old jacket); and a large black iron kettle steaming away on the coal bogie, seemed to be the most important items of gear on board – anything else was simply 'boat'.

On rare occasions, and to our utmost delight, those unique 'men of the sea' actually came ashore and visited our home, to return thanks for the gracious flow of

Mythology, Fantasy

hospitality. Inevitably, after the usual round of polite enquiries as to the well-being of friends and neighbours, and long discussions about weather and fishing in general, the conversation would turn to stories of times past, and strange tales of the sea.

Sruth na Fir Ghorm, the Stream of the Blue Men, a seething maelstrom between the Isles of Shiant and the eastern coast of the Isle of Lewis from Loch Bhrollum to Kebock Head, is one of those places where sometimes very, very strange things happened. There is always a nervous expectation of encountering the sombre unknown when sailing through *Sruth na Fir Ghorm*; but our visitors' narrative tonight is singularily strange, almost beyond belief.

Whilst fishing close to the boiling billows of *Sruth na Fir Ghorm*, the crew of a Scalpay boat came across what appeared to be a creature of human form, floating half out of the water. The *duine mara*, or merman, was known to have appeared to others in these waters, but here for the first time in their whole experience at sea, and, with the prospect of being ridiculed by all the rest of the island's fishermen, this crew were faced with the choice of either totally ignoring something extraordinary and now very close to them, or of taking the chance of obtaining at least some evidence of this alien encounter. With some difficulty, the creature was laid hold of and dragged out of the water on to the deck of their boat. For some time they studied their 'catch', which could only be explained, for the time being at least, as a *duine mara*. As they set out to secure the *duine mara* with a rope in order to ensure its safe arrival on Scalpay, they were all greatly distressed by the sudden appearance of another three similar creatures in the water close to their boat. Fearful now of being overwhelmed and themselves committed to the terrors of *Sruth na Fir Ghorm*, they released the captive *duine mara* who slithered eagerly over the side of the boat to join his companions in the sea, where they all disappeared from sight.

Mythology, Fantasy

Just a few years ago I had been relating the story of the 'Blue Men' to a mainland friend who was about to negotiate the 'stream' on his own for the very first time. He had no fears whatsoever. His boat 'Hurricane Jake' was big and powerful. Two thoroughbred diesel engines

Mythology, Fantasy

would propel her valiantly through the 'stream' in a matter of minutes, and this certainly was the case on the outward leg of the voyage from South Harris to Stornoway. In flat calm and at slack water Hurricane Jake literally flew over the watery abode of the Blue Men. Returning two days later was an entirely different matter – the Blue Men were lying in wait! Fiercely agitated by a stiff nor'-easter blowing against a powerful ebb tide, and no doubt seeking revenge for previously taking them by surprise, the Blue Men were now rearing upwards, their horrible bluey-green faces unveiled by the chill wind which whipped their frothy white locks and carelessly combined them with the flying spindrift which absolutely obliterated everything downwind. Viciously glinting eyes and dripping jabbering tongues were hurling salty contempt at Hurricane Jake, which by this time was reduced to a violent jolting and making an eternally slow passage through a brisk game of headers in the aquatic playing-field of the Blue Men. It was a badly bruised and deeply humiliated Alan who came ashore at Flodabay that evening – but I do believe there was just a hint of pride for Hurricane Jake who, after all, had won the day. And yes, robbed of his previous scepticism he ruefully admitted, 'Aye! that was some battle with the Blue Men of the Shiants today.'

There have been numerous accounts from every maritime nation, and, from all times throughout the history of the world, of strange creatures which inhabit the dark depths of the ocean. If not entirely destitute of truth, most of them largely owe their interest to the liberal embellishment with which they have been recorded. For a truly imaginative explanation of how these creatures exist in their submarine environment, and of how they are able to adapt to the terrestrial biosphere, we should go back to Samuel Hibbert, writing about the 'Superstitions of the Shetland Seas' in 1822:

> Of mermen and merwomen, many strange stories are told. Beneath the ocean, an atmosphere exists adapted

Mythology, Fantasy

to the respiring organs of certain beings, resembling, in form, the human race, who are possessed of surpassing beauty, of limited supernatural powers, and liable to the incident of death. They dwell in a territory of the globe far below the region of fishes, over which the sea, like the cloudy canopy of our sky, loftily rolls, and they possess habitations constructed of the pearly and coraline productions of the ocean. Having lungs not adapted to a watery medium, but to the nature of atmospheric air, it would be impossible for them to pass

Mythology, Fantasy

through the volume of waters that intervenes between the submarine and supra-marine world, if it were not for the extraordinary power that they inherit, of the entering the skin of some animal capable of existing in the sea, which they are enabled to occupy by a sort of demonaical possession. One shape that they put on, is that of an animal human above the waist, yet terminating below in the tail and fins of a fish, but the most favourite form is of the larger seal or Haaf-fish; for, in possessing an amphibious nature they are enabled not only to exist in the ocean, but to land on some rock, where they frequently lighten themselves of their sea-dress, resume their proper shape, and with much curiousity examine the nature of the upper world belonging to the human race. Unfortunately, however, each merman or merwoman, possesses but one skin, enabling the individual to ascend the seas, and if, on visiting the abode of man the garb should be lost, the hapless being must unavoidably become an inhabitant of our earth.

Samuel Hibbert's curiosity was indeed aroused, for (at immense risk to his own life) he landed 'not without considerable difficulty, on one of the rocks that forms a part of the Skerries, seven or eight miles north-west of Papa Stour', to see for himself the habitat of the Haaf-fish. The Ve Skerries are the haunt of a great many seals which in the past were hunted for their skins by the natives of Papa Stour. According to local folklore the Ve Skerries are:

> ... the particular retreat of the fair sons and daughters of the sea, where they are defended by a raging surf, that continually beats around them, from the obtrusive gaze and interference of mortals; here they release themselves from the skins within which they are inthralled, and, assuming the most exquisite human forms that ever were opposed to earthly eyes, inhale the upper atmosphere destined for the human race, and, by the moon's bright beams, enjoy their midnight revels.

Mythology, Fantasy

There appears to be a definite distinction made by some folklorists between the Fin-folk and the Seal-folk or 'Selchie', and in *The folklore of Orkney and Shetland*, Ernest W. Marmele highlights this disparity:

> The curious race of sea folk known as Fin Folk seems to belong specifically to the northern isles. In Shetland, Fin Folk and Seal Folk were frequently confused, and even regarded as the same beings, but in Orkney they were completely distinguished. The fact that they had farms on islands beneath the sea, and the circumstance that the beautiful mermaid was included in the Fin family, would suggest that they were related to those creatures of Norwegian legend, now forgotten in the islands, the huldrefolk. What makes things more confusing is that, in both groups of islands, the Fin Folk were sometimes thought of as sea monsters who took on the guise of marine animals and pursued fishing boats.

It is of quite some significance that the word huldrefolk in the Old Norse tongue suggests something or someone that is clothed with another skin. The O.N. *hulda* means a cover or sheath; and since those 'creatures of Norwegian legend' were recognised as being quite distinct from ordinary people, they were obviously regarded as not entirely belonging to the human race. The ability to take on 'the guise of marine animals' is quite intriguing, in view of the description that follows which indicates they must have used some kind of boat in contrast to the other 'sea-creatures' of aquatic lore: 'The Orkney Fin Man could row to Norway with seven *warts* (strokes) of the oar; but in this his Shetland equivalent surpassed him, for he could pull 50 miles a *tjoga* (a pull of the oar).' If they were indeed absolute sea-creatures, why should it be necessary for them to utilise a 'human' contrivance like an oar? And why should the extraordinary prowess of these apparently supernatural creatures be expressed in such a human way?

Mythology, Fantasy

The mythological Seal-folk, or the Selchie as they are sometimes known, on the other hand, were commonly recognised as being the subject of metamorphoses. The Grey Seals only, at certain times of the year, on shedding their skins became human beings, sharing their existence for a time with the ordinary people. F. Marian McNeill, whether by accident or by design, successfully combines most, if not all, of the various elements recognised in the Shetland 'Seal-folk' tradition, and expresses these by drawing on Jessie Saxby's profound perception of local lore. She is possibly taking us back even further in time, but yet there is sufficient similarity in those basic elements of that tradition for us to seek a common origin; for she states that:

> The elves and trolls of Scandinavian tradition differ considerably from the fairies of the Celtic tradition ... In Shetland, there lingers a tradition of a race called the 'peerie (little) hill-men', who inhabited the islands before either Pict or Norseman. They are thought to have been akin to the Lapps or 'Yaks' (Esquimaux), and 'from these' says Mrs. Saxby, the Shetland folklorist, 'comes without doubt our tradition of the Trows.' Later came the 'Muckle Maisters,' the Finns and Picts. The Finns are said to have had magical gifts, including the power to transform themselves into otters and seals. Hence, doubtless, the tradition of the 'Children of Lochlann,' the seal-folk of Hebridean folklore.
>
> *The Silver Bough*

Shetland has also given us the most famous of all songs or poems featuring the various legends of mermaids, seal-folk, and other fabulous inhabitants of the deep. In the ancient ballad of the Great Silkie of Sule Skerry we have a distinct illustration of the familiar image projected in Island folklore. The ballad now appears in various forms, but was originally written down by the antiquarian and naval hydrographer Captain Frederick Thomas, exactly as it was told to him

Mythology, Fantasy

by 'a venerable lady of Snarra Voe, Shetland', and recorded in the 1852 *Proceedings of the Society of Antiquaries of Scotland*. A 'Scottish' version was subsequently reprinted in Colburn's New Monthly Magazine in April 1864. It is reproduced here as it appears in F.J. Child's collection.

> An eartly nourris sits and sings,
> And aye she sings, Ba, lily-wean!
> Little ken I my bairnis father,
> Far less the land that he staps in.
>
> Then ane arose at her bed-fit,
> An a grumly guest I'm sure was he:
> 'Here am I, thy bairnis father,
> Although that I be not comelie.
>
> 'I am a man, upo the lan,
> And I am a silkie in the sea;
> And when I'm far and far frae lan,
> My dwelling is in Sule Skerrie.'
>
> 'It was na weel,' quoth the maiden fair,
> 'It was na weel, indeed,' quo she,
> 'That the Great Silkie of Sule Skerrie
> Suld hae come and aught a bairn to me.'
>
> Now he has taen a purse of goud,
> And he has put it upo her knee,
> Saying, Gie to me my little young son,
> An tak thee up thy nourris-fee.
>
> An it sall come to pass on a simmer's day,
> When the sin shines het on evera stane,
> That I will tak my little young son,
> An teach him for tae swim the faem.
>
> An thu sall marry a proud gunner,
> An a proud gunner I'm sure he'll be,
> An the very first schot that ere he schoots,
> He'll schoot baith my young son and me.

Mythology, Fantasy

It would be strange indeed if one of the greatest collectors and authors of fairy-tales had ignored the popular maritime traditions of his own time. Jakob Ludwig Grimm described the 'Finns' as beings which 'act just like men and women.' He said that they were 'like the swan-maidens and mer-wives of Scandinavian and German tradition, they are denizens of a region below the depths of the ocean, and are able to ascend to the land above by donning a seal-skin. If this integument be taken away from them, they cannot pass through the sea again and return to their proper abode.'

Equally perplexing is the reputation attached to one small isolated part of the Hebrides. Almost one mile along the coast from the northernmost tip of the Isle of Lewis, is this small islet – or almost an islet – since it remains connected, apart from periods of very high tides, by a narrow strip of rock to the rest of Lewis. It has puzzled historians and folklorists on account of its distinction of allegedly having been home to a tribe of diminutive people, or pygmies. This is *Luchruban*, or the 'Pygmies' Isle'. The earliest reference, and possibly the first instance of applying an English translation to the local Gaelic name, was by Dean Monro in 1549 whose interpretation 'Pygmeis Ile' has probably established an element of the extraordinary rather than simply describing a people of smaller stature than the indigenous population – 'Many men of different countries have delved deeply the floor of the little kirk, and I myself among the rest, and have found in it, deep under the earth, certain bones and round heads of wonderful little size, alleged to be the bones of the said pigmies.' If we take the name 'Ylen Dunibeg' as inscribed by the cartographer Pont around 1600, we find it is a good phonetic rendering of the Gaelic *Eilean nan Daoine Beag*, which is quite plainly and literally 'the Island of

Mythology, Fantasy

Small People'. In his *Description of Lewis* (1630), Captain Dymes describes this islet:

> Aboute a mile distant from this Chappell [SAINT MOLUIDH, EOROPIE], lyeth the Pygmeys Island wch is a round high hill contening about one acre of land. This Ile is ioyned to the Leweis by a narrow necke of land, wch is in length about half the distance of a paire of Butts, wherein there is the walls of a Chappell to bee seene wch is but 8 foote in length and 6 foote in breadth, the ground whereof hath bene often tymes digged vpp espetially by the Irish [THE GAELIC SPEAKING NATIVES OF LEWIS] wch come thither of purpose to gett the bones of those little people wch they say were buryed there. At my beinge vpon the Ile I made search in the earth and found some of those bones, wch are soe little that my beleife is scarce bigg enough to thinke them to bee the bones humane flesh.

This same island is later referred to by Martin Martin:

> The Ifland of *Pigmies*, or, as the natives call it, The *I land of Little Men*, is but of fmall extent. There has been many fmall Bones dug out of the Ground here, refembling thofe of Human Kind more than any other. This gave ground to a Tradition which the Natives have of a very Low-ftatur'd People living once here, call'd *Lusbirdan*, i.e. *Pigmies*.

Strangely enough Martin makes a similar reference to 'little people' on the Isle of Colonsay, when describing the fort (or *dùn*) of Dun-Evan. He says,

> ... the natives have a Tradition among them, of a very little Generation of People, that lived once here, call'd *Lusbirdan*, the fame with *Pigmies*.

It is a further cause for conjecture as to why we are now presented with another form of name by Martin even if it does mimic the earlier identities. In exploring the etymology of those names referred to above, the nearest equivalent to Martin's version is to be found in Ireland, and that being their word for 'little people' – Leprechaun – which itself is derived from the Old Irish,

Mythology, Fantasy

luchorpán, being from *lu*, small, and *corpan*, *corp*, a body. The modern Irish Gaelic version is *leipreachán*. Either of these two words can be seen as quite readily lending themselves to corruption, resulting in the *Lusbirdan* of Martin Martin, and in the name *Luchruban* as acknowledged in Lewis. It is still quite puzzling as to how Martin was not able to use the Lewis form of the name, since he was quite knowleable, if not fluent, in Gaelic.

The noted Hebridean historian William Cook Mackenzie also recognised this affinity with the ancient Irish tongue when he referred to the name 'Luchruban' on O.S. maps early this century- 'In the Ordnance Survey map of the present day [1905], it appears as 'Luchruban', which is plainly identical with *Luchorpáin*, or *Luchrupáin*, the diminutive people of Irish legend.' He also, in relating Dr. Beddoe's description of one type of the Lewis people, poses the question 'Have we here the descendants of the so-called pigmies?' Beddoe described them as 'a short, thick-set, snub-nosed, dark-haired, and even dark-eyed race', suggesting that they were probably aboriginal, and possibly Finnish.

The meaning of this name *Luchruban*, in its various forms, easily conforms to the physiognomy of the rumoured inhabitants of the small islet – *bodaich bheaga Luchruban* (the little men of *Luchruban*) – as they are still referred to in the Ness district of Lewis; and furthermore, it lends itself quite readily to association with the earliest reports of the Finn-folk, or Lapps, in Northern Norway. They are described by Claudius Clausson (1430), as 'the Wild Lapps' who 'are little pygmies ... whom I have seen ... taken at sea in a little hide-boat.' This particular people are also described by Michel Beheim (1450) and by Archbishop Walkendorf (1520) as 'short people ... who live in underground houses.'

W.C. Mackenzie coincidentally links his observations on Luchruban and its supposed inhabitants with the

Mythology, Fantasy

common northern Lewis traditions of fairy folklore. He recalls one of the Gaelic names given to the fairies, *Muinntir Fionnlagh,* or Finlay's people, and apparently for no other reason tenders this theory as offering another pathway to the tradition of Finn people in the Islands: 'I venture to suggest that this name means 'the little Finn people,' and that it links the Finnish aborigines with the 'good little people' of fairy lore who dwell in the bowels of green hills like Luchruban, and practise uncanny arts like the Lapp wizards.'

Archaeological investigation of the site on Luchruban by a brother and a cousin of Mackenzie revealed a quantity of bird and animal bones, some peat-ash, and a few pieces of unglazed, unfired pottery ornamented in a geometric pattern with bands of diagonal, parallel grooves. A detailed description by them of the remains of the building clearly implies its use as a place of habitation similar to that discovered on Eilean Mor in the Flannan Isles.

Why should anyone want to spend any length of time in this place, and how did they survive? To satisfy my own curiousity and interest, I ventured there in late April of this year, 1998. Walking west from the red brick Butt of Lewis lighthouse along vertical sea cliffs of about sixteen to twenty metres in height, one immediately feels a powerful sense of isolation – to the south and east of you is the whole of Europe, whilst to the north and west there is nothing but ocean as far as the eye can see. Isolation, that is apart from the birds. Rock face ledges are lined with row upon row of nesting gulls and fulmars; sea washed skerries far below are lined with the vertical figures of cormorants, evenly spaced like the teeth of a gigantic saw. On the cliff top edge, hungry ravens keep a watchful eye on the scene below, their glossy black plumage contrasting sharply with the flashing white of gannets plunging into the depths of the ocean beyond them.

Mythology, Fantasy

Luchruban still remains firmly attached to the rest of Lewis; but its land bridge lies at the bottom of an inhospitable rock chasm with vertical walls about fourteen metres high on either side. It is perfectly protected on all sides, a natural fortress; jagged sea stacks and skerries stand off from the base of its overhanging sea cliffs, and on the calmest of days the powerful tidal stream and ocean swell continue to crash against the menacing rocks. There is only one point of entry, that is from the landward side, and from a position where it would be quite impossible to approach unseen. The most primitive weapon would suffice to deter an invader.

A reasonably easy descent from the top of the landward cliff is possible at one place only, down a steep declivity of broken rock, so long as the greatest care is taken to avoid setting the whole lot in motion. After that, a short crossing ('half the distance of a pair of Butts') over several large pieces of fallen stone takes you to the base of the climb up the solid rock wall of Luchruban. This again for a fit person with the proper footwear is

Mythology, Fantasy

relatively easy on a calm day and in dry conditions, but I can imagine that when saturated with rain or sea spray, the smooth rock could be quite treacherous.

Over the top, and your feet are immediately sinking into the most luxuriant carpet of thick moss enriched with all manner of maritime vegetation – and straight away you are virtually knocking on the front door of the *bodaich bheaga*! The ruined walls of the ancient building are only three or four metres away from the top of the precipitous access route: instantly and totally defensible at this one point. Access by any other means or direction would be extremely hazardous.

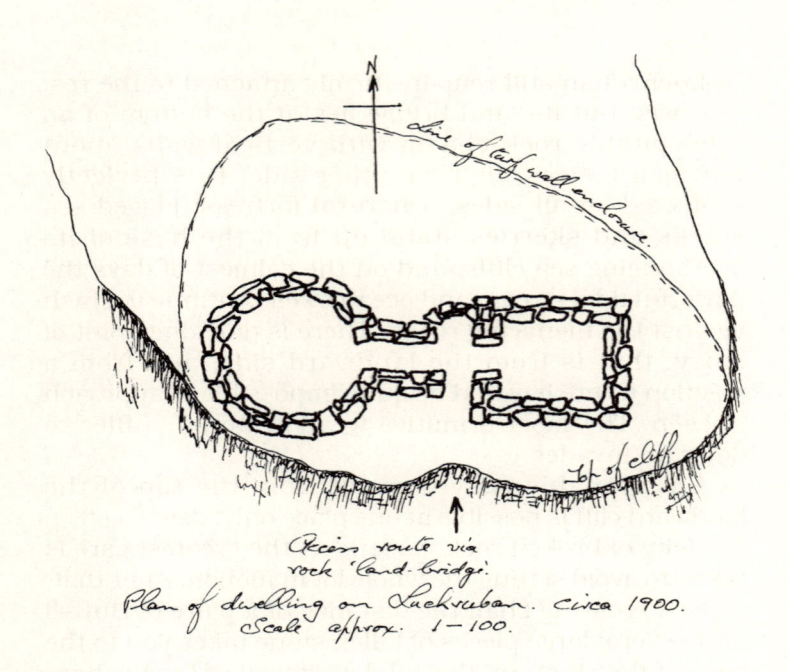

Plan of dwelling on Luckruban. circa 1900. Scale approx. 1–100.

Mythology, Fantasy

It is easy to imagine the ruined structure in its original habitable condition, with the main walls sunk about one metre below the level of the ground, that is, to the present floor level; and with its cantilevered stone roof well turfed over and appearing only as a small hillock on the otherwise flat plateau. Perfectly safe in all weather conditions, even though it obviously meant at times having to remain indoors for days on end during stormy weather – which is not unusual in the Hebrides, in our own time. Even at this height above sea level, in severe storms the sea breaking against the solid cliffs is forced upwards and then driven inland for some distance by the power of the wind.

Who then would want to make their home in such a place? A solitary monk in spiritual contemplation, as has been suggested? It is possible, though I doubt it very much. It would require an extremely fit and active person or persons to survive in such a place. The main food supply quite obviously would be seabirds and eggs taken from the cliffs, and just as it was on St. Kilda, fish would be less important even though it is there in abundance. The steep cliffs do not allow a safe landing to be made from a boat, and there is no place to keep any kind of craft safely here, not even a kayak, except further down the coast at the more easily accessible bay of Cunndal. Here, only ten minutes walk away, it is possible to launch and recover boats when the weather permits; and just above the beach there is evidence of a small settlement.

The seemingly precarious location of this ancient dwelling is really no different to many other isolated sites round the Island coasts and offshore islets where there is ample evidence of solitary ruins as well as those of larger settlements. I have absolutely no difficulty in accepting that it was perfectly feasible for someone to

Mythology, Fantasy

have lived on Luchruban for fairly long periods of time; and as Britt had said about the legendary inhabitants of Ha'sgeir – what else could they possibly need!

Yes, I did look for evidence of the little people, and luckily found some bones. I am now the proud owner of a skull from Luchruban. Well, it may have once been a fulmar – but who cares!

~ 5 ~

RECORDED EVENTS

Our skin-sewed Fin-boats lightly swim,
Over the sea like wind they skim.
Our ships are built without a nail;
Few ships like ours can row or sail.

Heimskringla

Every maritime nation has its very own typical Mermaid story, and all of them rightly are the subject, to a greater or lesser degree, of artistic or poetic embellishment. The difference in this account of the traditions of Seal-folk or Finn-folk in Scottish island folklore is that no attempt is made to enrich the factual content of individual sightings, neither is there any speculation as to the nature of the hidden parts, i.e., what remains unseen under the surface of the water.

We are all familiar with the distinctive 'Mermaid' description – half human and half fish; usually the upper half of a long haired female body as far as the waist, and with the lower part exactly like a fish, complete with a tail and scales.

Recorded Events

This in part is the likeness portrayed in the following account of several witnesses reported by Luke (Lucas) Jacobsøn Debes, who was 'Provost' of the Faroe churches.

> There was seen at Faroe, Westward of Wualboc Eide, by many of the inhabitants, as also by others from different parts of Suderoe, a Mer-maid close to the shore. She stood there two hours and a half, and was up to the navel in water. She had long hair on her head, which hung down to the surface of the water all round about her. She held a Fish, with the head downwards, in her right hand.

So goes the historical account of Luke Debes, translated from Danish into the English language in 1676. This, with the exception of the South Ronaldshay event, is possibly the earliest documentary evidence of the physical sighting of a 'Mermaid'; and although it is scant on detail, it nevertheless gives a full picture of what we have come to anticipate of such rare appearances.

There are three positive aspects to this account, which is in parallel with almost all other incidents reported in the traditions of Seal-folk. Firstly, the source is reasonably reliable. A person of such high standing in the church would definitely not jeopardise his position by falsely reporting the common account of several witnesses. Secondly, the description is sufficiently close to that of subsequently reported manifestations, that is, the upper half only, of a human body seen in an upright position in the water. Thirdly, despite calling her a mermaid he does not exaggerate on what was seen, or even speculate upon a supernatural source for the extraordinary appearance of such a being.

In examining all the available evidence from a variety of sources, those three points appear to be the key factors in establishing the credibility of witnesses to these events, whether from written evidence or oral folklore. It is also of great significance that this

Recorded Events

simplistic pattern to reported sightings of mer-folk occurs only within the area colonised by people who came exclusively from the northern regions of Norway: i.e. the Faroes, the Islands of Shetland, the Orkney Isles, the Hebrides, and the neighbouring mainland parts of northern and western Scotland.

For a typical report of strange sightings around Orkney and Shetland, and that same report from someone whose sole purpose was to examine the religious and moral state of the people thereof, we have the stories related by John Brand, following his visit to these islands. Brand was one of a party sent by the Church of Scotland to report on the northern limits of its area of responsibility as we see from the following extract from his book:

> Commiffion to Zetland.
>
> The General Assembly Anno 1700, upon the defire of certain minifters in Zetland, and Information of the State of Affairs in thefe remote Iflands, found it neceffary to depute a Commiffion thither, confifting of feven Minifters and one Ruling Elder; With Power not only to vifite and order the Churches there, but like wife to concur with and affift the Prefbyteries of Orkney and Caithnefs, as there should be occasion.

This intrepid body of Commissioners on behalf of the General Assembly of the Church of Scotland sailed from Leith on Friday the 12th of April, 1700, bound for Orkney and Shetland; arriving in Orkney on the following Monday afternoon. A fishing smack transported them thence throughout the Islands. John Brand, one of the ministers, on their return to Edinburgh, wrote a book describing their travels, and what they saw and heard therein; entitled *A New Description of Orkney, Zetland, Pightland Firth and Caithne s*. I have already mentioned his comment on the Norrn tongue being still in use, at that time, by the people in the Parish of Hara. He also wrote:

Recorded Events

There are frequently Fin-men seen here upon the Coasts, as one about a year ago on Stronsa, and another within these few months on Westra, a gentleman with many others in the Isle looking on him nigh to the shore, but when they endeavour to apprehend them they flee away most swiftly; which is very strange, that one man sitting in his little boat, should come some hundreds of leagues, from their own coasts, as they reckon Finland to be from Orkney. It may be thought wonderful how they live all that time, and are able to keep to sea so long. His boat is made of seal-skins, or some kind of leather; he also has a coat of leather upon him, and he sitteth in the middle of his boat, with a little oar in his hand, fishing with his lines. And when in a storm he seeth the high surge of a wave approaching, he hath a way of sinking his boat, till the wave passes over, lest thereby he should be overturned. The Fishers here observe that these Fin-men or Finland-men, by their coming drive away the fishes from the coasts. One of these boats is kept as a rarity in the Physicians Hall at Edinburgh.

About two years and a half or three years ago, there was a boat passing with several gentlemen of the Country in it, and by the way of the Voe of Quarf, through which they went, there appeared something unto them with its head above the water, which as they could discern had the face of an old Man, with a long beard hanging down; first it appeared at some distance from them, and then coming nearer to their boat, they had a clear sight of it; the sight was so strange and affrighting, that all in the Boat were very desirous to be on land, the day was fair and the sea calm; a gentleman declaring, (as a minister in the company with them, and saw this sight informed me,) that he never saw the like, tho he had travelled through many seas.

And again, he continues with another description on which possibly is founded the tale of the unfortunate mermaid who was caught on a fish-hook which was told by Jessie Saxby. This is how Brand describes the incident:

Recorded Events

About five years hence, a boat at the Fishing drew her lines, and one of them, as the Fishers thought, having some great fish upon it, was with greater difficulty than the rest raised from the Ground, but when raised it came more easily to the surface of the water upon which a creature like a woman presented itself at the side of the boat, it had the face, Arms, breasts, shoulders etc. of a woman, and long hair hanging down the back, but the nether part from below the breasts, was beneath the water, so that they could not understand the shape therof. The two fishers who were in the boat being surprised at this strange sight, one of them unadvisedly drew a knife, and thrust it into her breast, whereupon she cried, as they judged, <u>Alas,</u> and the hook giving way she fell backward and was no more seen: The hook being big went in at her chin and out at the upper lip. The man who thrust the knife into her is now dead, and, as was observed, never prospered after this, but was still haunted by an evil spirit, in the appearance of an old man, who, as he thought, used to say unto him, <u>'Will ye do such a thing who killed the Woman.'</u> The other man then in the boat is yet alive in the isle of Burra.'

    Hence are accounts given of those Sea Monsters, the Meerman and Meermaids, which have not only been seen but apprehended and kept for some time.

These extraordinary accounts are secondary to Brand's purpose in visiting Orkney and Shetland, and are not crucial elements in the content of his book; nevertheless they serve to highlight the importance of those incidents which the Rev. James Wallace described almost ten years earlier and further reinforce those with such details as Brand gleaned himself, for example, the sighting of Finmen near Stronsay and Westray.

    Alasdair Alpin Macgregor, or *Alasdair suarach* (loathsome Alasdair), a demeaning title he earned for merely reporting the truth about the native Hebrideans, wrote in one of his excellent books on the Hebrides about a 'canoe' hanging in the church of Burray in Orkney. Strangely, this particular specimen though

Recorded Events

contemporaneous with his visit to the northern isles is not mentioned by Brand. It does appear to be a genuine report, however, and quite separate from the kayak mentioned by Dr. James Wallace which was 'catched in Orkney' and subsequently bequeathed to Edinburgh University in 1696.

David MacRitchie considered it possible that the Burray canoe was the one referred to in the Kirk Session Record of South Ronaldshay and Burray in 1661. That record states that on Sunday 26th. May, 1661, in St. Peter's Kirk, South Ronaldshay, a collection of 16s. 6d. [82.5p.] was taken as 'charity to ane poore Yetland (i.e., Shetland) man whom God had wonderfully preserved into a storme at sea into his litill boate, and taken by ane vessell finding him upon the seas'. (See Dr. Craven's *Church Life in South Ronaldshay and Burray in the Seventeenth Century*, Kirkwall, 1911, p. 36.) MacRitchie comments,

> It is a little remarkable that a Shetlander would have been picked up by a vessel putting in at the most southern island of the Orkney group. Moreover, it is unlikely that a Shetlander of the ordinary type would be found adrift in Orkney waters in a small open boat, or that such a boat could weather a heavy storm. On the other hand, if the man was a Finman in his kayak, coming from Shetland, or describing himself as a Shetlander, the situation would be more easily understood. It might be conjectured that the recipient of the 16s. 6d. afterwards settled in the little island of Burray, across the narrow sound, and that thus his kayak was eventually preserved in the church of Burray. All this is conjecture, but the incident if 1661 seems deserving of mention in this connection.

The Rev James Wallace, a graduate of Aberdeen University and Minister of Kirkwall, whose son Dr. Wallace is referred to above, wrote *A Description of the Isles of Orkney* which was first published in 1693, five years after his death; and which, apart from the

Recorded Events

Ronaldshay account, contains what is probably the first Scottish record of these extraordinary events:

> Sometime about this country are seen those Men which are called 'Finmen'; in the year 1682 one was seen some time sailing, sometime rowing up and down in his little Boat at the south end of the Isle of Eda, most of the people of the Isle flocked to see him, and when they adventured to put out a boat with men to see if they could apprehend him, he presently sped away most swiftly: and in the year 1684, another was seen from Westra, and for a while after they got a few or no fishes: for they have this Remark here, that these 'Finmen' drive away the fishes from the place to which they come.

This brief note reflects most other descriptions of a 'Finman' in his little boat doing whatever they normally did; furthermore it implies that although such sightings were not exactly rare, they stirred up sufficient interest locally to be personally viewed by most of the islanders. Wallace, inferring an Eskimo origin, does suggest that 'these 'Finmen' seem to be some of these people that dwell about the Fretum Davis' (Davis Strait); yet he still uses the traditional local adjunct 'Finmen' which signifies none other but a Nordic source.

In the same period Martin Martin refers to these same incidents in both Orkney and Shetland, and says of Orkney:

> The Finland Fiſhermen have been frequently ſeen on the Coaſt of this Iſle, particularily in the Year 1682. The People on the Coaſt ſaw one of them in his little Boat, and endeavour'd to take him, but he could not come at him, he retired ſo ſpeedily. They ſay the Fiſh retire from the Coaſt, when they ſee theſe Men come to it.

Martin calls them 'Finland Fishermen'; once again acknowledging local tradition, but clearly not distinguishing between proven reality and the supernatural phenomena associated with those events, for in writing about Shetland, he recounts:

Recorded Events

There have been feveral ftrange Fifh feen by the Inhabitants of the Sea, fome of the Shape of Men as far as the Middle; they are both troublefom and very terrible to the Fifhers, who call them Sea-Devils.

The Bishop of Bergen, Erik Pontoppidan, a member of the Royal Academy of Sciences at Copenhagen, 'stoutly defended' the existence of the Mermaid, or Hav-Fruen, in his *Natural History of Norway* Vol. 11; – Hav-Manden and Hav-Fruen – 'are often, but not always, fabulous. They exist in fact, which is undeniably proved, both by evidence of our Norwegians and foreigners'.

The Shetland folklorist Robert Sinclair reinforces this statement of the Bishop of Bergen, in that he refers to Finns rowing between Shetland and the Norwegian town of Bergen. A certain Lieut. G.T. Temple, R.N. further suggested that an inlet at Bergen called 'Fens Fiord' may be associated with the Finns; and pointed to a special caste known as Strils who were very primitive in character, and who were regarded by the neighbouring Norwegians as of a different stock from their own, who still inhabited the numerous islands that protect Bergen from the ocean. 'They speak Norwegian after a fashion of their own, but it is very difficult to understand them, and there is reason to suppose that their idioms have a Samoyede root'. Temple tentatively placed these people linguistically within the circumpolar cultural area, but without identifying a particular race.

Nevertheless, there is almost sufficient evidence to establish the source of strange people appearing in the Scottish Islands. MacRitchie, who studied the kayak reports at length, and whose work we will later examine in detail, regards the possibility of Eskimoes crossing the North Atlantic as very remote – 'Indeed the feat is almost an impossibility. Moreover, it is quite clear that those Finn-men were frequent and voluntary visitors to the Orkneys, and (more especially) to the Shetlands; and the 'Fin-land' from which they come is stated by the Shetlanders to have been no further off than Bergen, on the Norwegian coast.'

Recorded Events

MacRitchie accepted that those visitations were as numerous as was reported from Shetland and Orkney, and indeed folklore supports this view, even far beyond those events which were 'officially' recorded. Moreover, he also conforms to the Shetlanders' assumption that these people crossed from Bergen. This is perfectly reasonable, knowing that the immediate area of Bergen is the shortest sea crossing between Norway and Shetland; and even if the kayakers' origin was much farther to the north, it would be quite logical to expect them to exploit the safety of the Norwegian coast as far south as Bergen before proceeding across the two hundred and twenty miles stretch of open sea to Shetland.

Only those several reports from around this particular time of people in kayaks appearing around Orkney and Shetland, along with one or two other isolated events, such as the one captured near Aberdeen, have been the basis of speculation as to their origin. This has always been founded on the individual kayak designs, rather than any study of the individuals 'captured' who were discounted as being Eskimos from Greenland. This is an odd conjecture, and obviously one that MacRitchie did not feel comfortable with. He argued strongly for the folklore element to be included in any study of kayaks and their occupants; and for this he has been severely criticised and even ridiculed by some for not conforming to accepted empirical methodology.

Also strongly supporting the relevance of traditional oral folklore to historical fact, the German folklorist and historian Dr. Karl Blind shrewdly pointed to the reality in which mythology is rooted when writing on the subject of 'sea-creatures':

> in Shetland, and elsewhere in the North, the sometimes animal-shaped creatures of this myth, but who in reality are human in a higher sense, are called Finns. Their transfiguration into seals seems to be more a kind of deception they practise. For the males are described as most daring boatmen, with powerful sweep of the

Recorded Events

oar, who chase foreign vessels on the sea. At the same time they are held to be deeply versed in magic spells and in the healing art, as well as in soothsaying. By means of a 'skin' which they possess, the men and women among them are able to change themselves into seals. But on shore, after having taken off their wrappage, they are, and behave like, real human beings. Any one who gets hold of their protecting garment has the Finn in his power. Only by means of the skin can they go back to the water. Many a Finn woman has got into the power of a Shetlander and borne children to him; but if a Finn woman succeeded in re-obtaining her sea-skin, or seal-skin, she escaped across the water. Among the older generation in the Northern Isles persons are still sometimes heard of who boast of hailing from the Finns; and they attribute to themselves a peculiar luckiness on account of their higher descent.

'Hailing from the Finns', or descended from the Seal-folk, is the best evidence we have at the present time, especially in the Hebrides, for making this vital connection between folklore and reality – and more so in directly attributing their roots to the people of Northern Norway. The MacCodrum family and others of similar pedigree are adequate proof of this affinity with a people from outwith their own immediate cultural region. It could be argued that they, like so many other islanders, were merely a remnant from the period of Norse occupation. That particular point, I am certain, is what adds strength to the argument rather than detracting from it, the very fact that our islands were home to the Norse people for a period of around five hundred years; and that during that time it would not be at all strange if a good many of those settlers were 'Lapps' originally from the far north of Norway.

There have been many other encounters with 'sea-creatures' which have not been specifically identified as kayakers, but are more in the way of being a part of traditional lore, or even mythology. However, several

Recorded Events

have been recorded by reliable witnesses, and even if there appears to be an element of the supernatural in some instances, the basic information is fairly consistent throughout and generally describes the upper half of a human form.

For a first-hand commentary of a personal encounter with a 'Mermaid', we must come across to the North coast of Scotland, where on the wild shores of the Pentland Firth a schoolmaster out for a walk was confronted with an extraordinary sight. On the 8th of September, 1809, there was a letter published in *The Times* written by Mr. William Munro, who quite understandably for someone of considerable standing in the locality, must have been extremely concerned at the prospect of being utterly ridiculed, when it took this length of time to testify publicly of his extraordinary encounter:

> About twelve years ago, when I was Parochial Schoolmaster at Reay, in the course of my walking on the shore at Sandside Bay, being a fine warm day in summer, I was induced to extend my walk towards Sandside Head, when my attention was arrested by the appearance of a figure resembling an unclothed human female, sitting upon a rock extending into the sea, and apparently in the action of combing its hair, which flowed around its shoulders, and of a light brown colour.

Mr. Munro was in no doubt as to the form of what he witnessed, and though he describes it in great detail, was unable to acknowledge it as being human – simply from its situation on a rock which he considered to be unsafe for bathing. He did extend his examination as far as the hands of the creature, but could not determine if the fingers were webbed or not. All the rest of its features were no different to any other human being. Mr. Munro, until this time, had been quite sceptical of all other reports of this nature, and even if it took him twelve years to testify publicly to what he

Recorded Events

saw, it left him in no doubt as to its existence, for he says:

> If the above narrative can in any degree be subservient towards establishing the existence of a phenomena hitherto almost incredible to naturalists, or to remove the scepticism of others. who are ready to dispute everything which they cannot fully comprehend, you are welcome to it,
>
> from, Dear Sir, Your most obliged, and most humble servant, William Munro.

Five years later, which is actually seventeen years since Mr. Munro's experience at Sandside Bay, yet another schoolmaster reports an unusual incident which startled two fishermen at sea. On the 20th August 1814, a letter from George MacKenzie, the schoolmaster at Rathven in Bannfshire, was printed; with the description of a merman and his mate which appeared to two fishermen of Portgordon, just to the west of the fishing port of Buckie.

> About three or four o'clock yesterday afternoon, (15th. August) when about a quarter of a mile from the shore, the sea being perfectly calm, they observed, at a small distance from their boat, with its back towards them, and half its body above the water, a creature of a tawny colour, appearing like a man sitting, with his body half bent.

This time the likeness was to a male, at least down to the waistline. The two fishermen furnished a good description of that part of the body above water, and even below the waist they described the body as tapering to a considerable length 'like a large fish without scales'. For some time they watched, and in turn were watched, till eventually the creature dived below the surface of the sea. When it reappeared a bit further away it was acompanied by another which was obviously female. They described her long hair and breasts. Anxious for their own safety, the two men rowed rapidly towards the shore, where news of their incredible encounter quickly

Recorded Events

spread around. Mr. MacKenzie who heard their story 'was sufficiently impressed with the character and integrity of the two fishermen who saw the creatures to take down their testimony, and to risk the charge of credulity by forwarding it to the local newspaper.'

Nearly all descriptions on record concern the adult of the species, and at no time has there been an authenticated examination of a dead body – except for one pathetic incident which, although phenomenal, merited the ordering of a decent burial by a person in a responsible position of authority.

About 1830, some crofter women, who had been harvesting seaweed on the shores of the island of Benbecula in the Outer Hebrides, told the story of how they had met a creature of the female form playing happily just off the shore. Sadly, only a few days later her dead body was picked up about two miles from where she had first been seen. The event is described thus:

> The upper portion of the creature was about the size of a well fed child of three or four years of age, with an abnormally developed breast. Hair long, dark and glossy, skin white, soft and tender. The lower part of the body like a salmon, but without scales. Crowds of people came to see it. Mr. Duncan Shaw, factor for Clanranald, Baron-baille and Sheriff of the district, ordered a coffin and shroud to be made for the mermaid. This was done and the body buried near the shore in the presence of many people. There are people still living [i.e. in the late nineteenth century] who saw and touched this curious creature and give graphic descriptions of its appearance.

It may be considered quite odd that in this report of a physical examination of one of those mysterious sea-creatures, we have a description of the lower half of the body 'like a salmon, but without scales'. This indicates, either a tail-like appendage, or else that both legs were contained in a common sleeve, which may not be

Recorded Events

inconceivable, if the juvenile 'creature' had just abandoned her own kayak, and was still wearing a garment designed for such use.

If we consider the huldrefolk mentioned by Marmele, and the significance of some kind of cover or sheath over part of the body, it is not difficult to equate this event with other incidents of sea-creatures and kayak users who were attributed with a tail-like appendage. It is extremely unlikely that any detailed examination was carried out, or even more than a cursory inspection by Mr. Shaw. Common superstition and fear of the unknown would have been sufficient to protect the modesty of the moment, and to preserve forever the secret of the unfortunate child.

Another time a diminutive 'lady' of the sea, with quite peculiar capabilities, was examined at length on board a fishing vessel. The incident was of sufficient credibility for the information to be relayed by a Mr. Edmonston to the Professor of Natural History at the University of Edinburgh.

Recorded Events

In 1833 six Shetland fishermen, working off the Isle of Yell, on returning to land reported that their lines had got entangled with a mermaid. They had kept this creature, which they estimated to be about three feet long, on board the boat for three hours. She 'offered no resistance nor attempted to bite', but kept on moaning piteously. 'A few stiff bristles were on the top of her head, extending down to the shoulders, and these she could erect and depress at pleasure, something like a crest.' This mermaid had neither gills nor fins, and there were no scales on her body. The superstitious fishermen threw her overboard eventually and related that she dived 'in a perpendicular direction'. Mr. Edmonston who had this story from the Skipper and crew says that 'not one of the six men dreamed of a doubt of its being a mermaid,' and furthermore states that fear would not have so clouded their reasoning as to result in an error of judgement.

In this instance, the physical description is vague, or even totally lacking any human qualities, so it is quite difficult to say with any degree of certainty if this was indeed a being of human form. It may well have been an unusual type of fish, or a mutant of a better known specimen; once again a combination of superstition and fear would serve to prevent a close investigation – better to return it to the deep rather than risk the consequences of tampering with the unknown!

From much further south now, in the Kintyre peninsula, we have two separate reports of what appears in all likelihood to have been the same subject viewed by different people. This incident aroused sufficient interest to have the witnesses examined in the presence of Duncan Campbell, Esq., Sheriff-substitute of Campbeltown.

John M'Isaac, a local farmer, was sworn in and testified to his observing of a 'sea-creature' for nearly two hours. He was cross-examined and remained firm

Recorded Events

in his belief of what he saw. That on the twenty-ninth of October, 1811 he had been walking by the sea-shore and noticed something unusual upon a rock in the sea. He stated 'That the upper half of it was white, and of the shape of a human body, and the other half towards the tail of a brindled reddish-grey colour apparently covered with long hair.' Once again we have this impression of a 'tail', which Mr. M'Isaac said was extended like a fan and moving about 'in tremulous motion'. The 'animal' had all the appearance of a human being, but from the middle down the body tapered gradually to the point of the tail. It had also been seen on the same day by some boys near by.

Recorded Events

Appearing before Sheriff Campbell four days later was Katherine Loynachan, daughter of a herdsman in the same district, who had three weeks earlier witnessed a similar creature on a rock near the shore. It slid off the rock and disappeared under water coming up again about six yards further out. Again it was described as of human form, but with the body 'tapering like a fish,' in fact she took it to be a boy who somehow had fallen off a ship. In both cases the descriptions are sufficiently close to be describing, if not the same, then two separate but very similar persons probably in a kayak. The tapering tail, which is the only non human element, as seen from a distance, and the actions of each both on the rock and in the water would be consistent with what you would expect of a kayaker launching into the sea. Their testimonies, despite Mr. M'Isaac being within 'twelve or fifteen paces' are insufficient to reach any conclusion. They do however support the evidence of other sightings, far enough removed from the same area not to have been influenced by them.

Having wandered as far south as the Kintyre peninsula, it is well worth while going slightly further afield, and even further back in time, to consider the story of a 'sea-man' captured off the Yorkshire coast, near Skinningrave, in 1535, as described by the Rev. John Graves in his 'History of Cleveland' (1808):

> Camden mentions the report of a *sea-man* being caught by the fishermen here; and the same fabulous story is thus more particularily related in the ancient M.S. above quoted [M.S. in Cott. Library, marked Julius F.C. fol. 455]: 'Old men would be loath to have their Credyt crackt by a Tale of a stale Date, report confidently that sixty Yeares since, or perhaps 80 or more, a *sea-man* was taken by the Fishers of that place [Skinningrave], where duringe many weeks they kepte in an oulde House, giving him rawe Fishe to eate, for all other fare he refused; insteade of Voyce he shreeked, and shewed

Recorded Events

himself courteous to such as flocked farre and neare to visit him; – fayre Maydes were wellcomest Guests to his Harbour, whom he woulde beholde with a very earneste Countenaynce, as if his phlegmaticke Breaste had been touched wth a Sparke of Love. – One Day, when the good Demeanour of this newe Gueste had made his Hosts secure of his Abode wth them, he privately stoale out of Doores, and ere he coulde be overtaken recovered the Sea, whereinto he plounged himself; – yet as one that woulde not unmannerly depart without taking his Leave, from the mydle upwardes he raysed his Shoulders often above the Waves, and makinge signes of acknowledging his good Enterteinment to such as beheld him on the Shore, as they interpreted yt; – after a pretty while he dived downe and appeared no more.'

In quoting this tale in 'The Kayak in North-Western Europe', Macritchie goes on to comment:

In his 'History of Whitby' (Whitby, 1817, p. 798), Young suggests that this 'sea-man' may have been a seal. This idea may find support from the manner of his final disappearance. It is a fact, also, that seals eat their fish raw. On the other hand, a seal could hardly live in a house for many weeks without water to bathe. Moreover, it may be questioned whether a captive seal on the Yorkshire coast in the sixteenth century would attract people from far and near; nor is it likely that a seal would pay special attention to 'fayre maydes'. Much more might be said in favour of the view that this 'sea-man' was of the same kind as the Orkney Finmen of the seventeenth century, and that he made his escape by retrieving his captured kayak, although the traditional account speaks of his diving under water like a marine animal. Apparently the story was not recorded in writing until eighty years after the event, by which time the details may have become blurred in the popular memory.

This date in which the story was recorded, eighty years on, coincides with the acquisition of a kayak by Trinity House in Hull in the year 1613, which is referred

Recorded Events

to by Gert Nooter (*Old Kayaks in the Netherlands*) as unlikely to be made from whalebone, as was claimed. But he was unable at that time to make a close examination. However he does state, confirming the measurements given by Souter, that it was made for a young man. It is described in the following chapter.

~ 6 ~

KAYAKS

Like a weavers shuttle

Sir Nicolo Zeno

Professor Nicolay Nicolaysen, writing in 1882, referred to Bronze Age rock carvings called 'Helleristninger' with representations of ancient boats which appear to have a keel in one piece, 'while the ribs consisted of withies covered with skins, such as the boats of the Esquimaux, or the so-called hudkeipr used by our ancestors'.

The Old Norse word *húð-keipr* aptly describes the skin-covered canoe or kayak: from *húð* (hide), and *keipr* (sledge runner), describing the material used in the covering, as well as the distinctive shape of the boat. This basic description also implies flexibility and speed, very desirable characteristics for a craft that operates in conditions where a normal boat just could not survive. Manoeuvering amongst skerries and shoals in strong tides and severe weather, and being able to 'haul out' like a seal on to seaweed covered rocks, would destroy the best wooden boat in a very short time.

The question of frailty, as so frequently implied, is negated in the description of the Greenland kayaks by Jens Kreutzmann: 'The elongated, slim shape would indicate frailness, but that is not the case. The kayak is designed for maximum strength. The components of the kayak's wooden hull, or skeleton, link up and intertwine in a way that permits all parts to give without breaking up ... This combination of a flexible skeleton and a strong water-resistant cover gives the kayak its strength.'

Kayaks

The earliest example of a 'kayak' preserved as a trophy in a European church is furnished by Dr. Nansen. It is of the year 1430. The chronicler is a certain Dane named Claudius Clausson, or Clavus, who informs us that to the west of the Wild Lapps '... are little pygmies, a cubit high, whom I have seen,' he affirms, 'after they were taken at sea in a little hide-boat, which is now (about 1430) hanging in the cathederal at Nidaros [TRONDHEIM] There is likewise', he goes on to say, 'a long vessel of hides, which was also once taken with such Pygmies in it'.

Dr. Nansen also cites Michel Beheim, who travelled in Norway in 1450. There he saw or heard of a people called 'Skraelings' who are only three 'spans' high, but are nevertheless dangerous opponents both on sea and land. 'They live in caves which they dig out in the mountains, make ships of hides, eat raw meat and raw fish, and drink blood with it.' Then there is the similar testimony by Archbishop Erik Walkendorf, who, in his description of Finmark, written about 1520, says: 'Finmark has on its north-north-west a people of short and small stature, namely, a cubit and a half, who are commonly called 'Skraelinger'; they are an unwarlike people, for fifteen of them do not dare approach one Christian or Russian either for combat or parley. They live in underground houses, so that one neither can examine them nor capture them.' A notable difference however exists in those descriptions, and that lies in the conflicting accounts of the primitive disposition of the 'Skraelings'. Beheim, who was obviously from a more 'refined' society, suggests a rather barbarous race, whilst Walkendorf describes them as 'unwarlike'. This peaceable nature accords well with the Sami traditions, whose language contains no words that describe war.

Like the Welsh coracle and the Irish *curragh* of the early Celtic people, the kayak appears to have been a refinement of the basic 'hide covered wooden frame' type of open boat, adapted to operate in specific conditions,

Kayaks

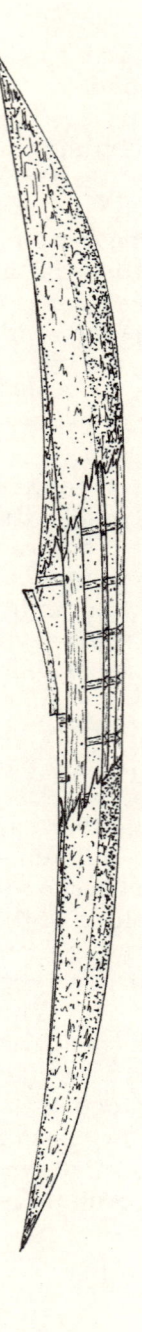

and, with several unique characteristics which are not replicated in our modern versions of canoe or kayaks.

David MacRitchie conveniently uses the word *kayak* 'in its common acceptance as denoting the long, narrow, skin-covered canoe of the Eskimo', sometimes varying into *kyak, kayik,* or *kayook*. He also refers to 'a people in the north-west of Norway known as 'Skraelings' who made use of skin boats and lived in caves and underground houses' as users of kayaks. He goes on to say, 'It will be remembered that this name 'Skraeling' was applied by the Norsemen to the Eskimo whom they encountered in North America in the eleventh century. They sometimes referred to them also as 'Lapps', and at other times as 'trolls.' There is no evidence that those Eskimo represented a type of man previously unknown to the Norsemen.'

MacRitchie appends his paper with the excellent description by R.W. Reid (at that time, 1912, Professor of Anatomy at Aberdeen University and Curator of the Anthropological Museum) of the kayak which was taken with its occupant near Aberdeen, and given to the Anthropological Museum of Marischal College about the beginning of the eighteenth century. At the time, the kayak, and its unfortunate occupant who died after only three days in captivity, was thought to have come from Greenland, or even from Labrador.

Kayaks

Professor Reid's measurements may appear a little cumbersome, having both Metric and Imperial equivalents further complicated with unusual fractions of inches; but it is important to follow the same detail which he set out.

The general appearance of the *kayak* is well seen in the accompanying illustrations (Plate xxxvi). It measures 5,400 mm.(17 feet 9 inches) in length, 450 mm.(1 foot 5 3/4 inches) in its greatest breadth, and 230 mm.(9 1/8 inches) in its greatest depth. It weighs, without implements, 15.4 kilograms (34 pounds). Its bottom is flat, excepting for the distance of about 760 mm.(2 feet 5 7/8 inches) from its bow and 660 mm.(2 feet 2 inches) from its stern, where it gradually rises to the pointed ends of the kayak. The deck is flat, with the exception of the extremities, which are very slightly elevated, and it presents a little behind its middle a nearly circular aperture – manhole – measuring 400 mm.(1 foot 3 3/4 inches) in its antero-posterior and 385 mm.(1 foot 3 1/8 inches) in its transverse diameter. Immediately behind the manhole are two strips of hide, each of an average diameter of 6 mm.(1/4 inch) attached to the margins of the kayak and crossing the upper surface of the deck. The strips are arranged in such a way that the one next the manhole passes through a slit in the one next the stern, so as to give the general appearance of a crossing in the middle line 205 mm.8 1/10 inches) behind the manhole. About 450 mm.(1 foot 5 3/4 inches) in front of the manhole a single strip of hide, attached to the edges of the boat, crosses the deck transversely.

The kayak is made of four seal skins stretched over a slender framework of wood. The skins have their subcutaneous surfaces next to the cavity of the kayak. Their edges are overlapped and sewed together with strips of tendon, in such a way as to produce a neat, smooth, flat and very strong seam. The only seams in the bottom and sides of the kayak are those which join the skins transversely. Seams in other directions, chiefly longitudinal, exist in the deck only. The framework is made of pieces of redwood, which average

Kayaks

about 27 mm.(1 1/10 inches) in breadth by 19 mm.(19/25 inch) in thickness, and are lashed together by strips of whalebone and hide.

Bounding the manhole is a wooden girth which was inserted in 1900 to replace the original girth, which had become so decayed that it crumbled away. It is lashed to the adjacent seal-skin deck by a hempen rope which

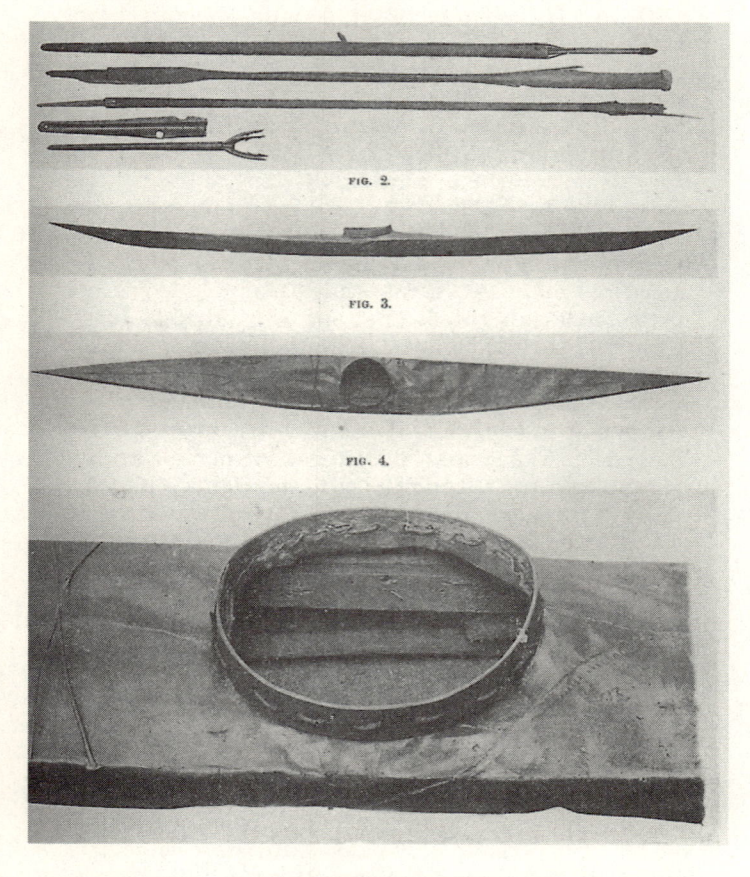

Photograph accompanying Professor Reid's article in *Journal of the Royal Anthropological Institute of Great Britain and Ireland*, vol. xlii, 1912.

Kayaks

at the same date was inserted to replace the original strip of hide which had been used for the purpose. Three pieces of timber are seen through the manhole with iron nails piercing one of them. These are not the original timbers, but were also inserted in 1900 in order to strengthen the framework of the kayak.

A report, from round about the same time, on the wood framing of the kayak, and its implements, is furnished by Mr. William Dawson, B.Sc., Lecturer in Forestry in the University of Aberdeen. In this he states that all the wood in the framework of the kayak (excepting the repairs done in Aberdeen, 1900), is of *Pinus silvestris*, known in this country as Scots fir, and, according to Mr. Dawson, native to Northern Europe. Moreover he states:

> The wood of the spears in the Aberdeen kayak, shows the character of timber grown in a continental climate, and that, too, in a continental climate pretty far north or at very high elevation. The characters from which this can be deduced are (1) the extreme regularity of each season's growth, and (2) the smallness of each season's growth. Wood grown in an insular climate shows less regularity, due to the prevelance of spring frosts after growth has begun, and the consequent checking of the development of the wood, and also shows greater growths in each year owing to the longer growing season. The wood of these spears is similar in character to some of the wood we get at the present time from Norway and Sweden and from Finland, but is not similar to anything produced in this country, even in the remains of the native forests. The thrower (a small piece of wood for launching the spears) is of wider ringed wood, but it, too, is regularly grown, and might have been grown in more sheltered places in the same neighbourhood as produced the wood of the spears. The Pinus silvestris is native over a considerable part of North and Middle Europe, but the Baltic neighbourhood is its principal habitat.

A Marischal College publication *Eskimo Kayaks in Aberdeen* furnishes a general description and photo-

Kayaks

graphs of one of the kayaks in their possession. There is no suggestion they could be any other than Eskimo kayaks of Greenland origin. It does refer to the Hull kayak as probably the oldest found in Britain, and, containing a dead paddler! The kayaks are described as follows:

> The frame is of driftwood carefully jointed and fitted together, with ivory or bone sometimes used for the reinforcement. Greased sealskins are sewn to the frame and regular applications of oil are needed to keep the hull waterproof and flexible. A central cockpit has a collar of wood or whalebone around which the kayaker's anorak can be sealed. With his hood and sleeves closed tight by drawstrings the paddler and his craft form a single watertight unit which can be safely capsized and rolled. The double paddle of wood has its slender blades reinforced with strips of bone.

Equipped for seal hunting, it would carry on its deck the harpoon and throwing-board, a stabbing spear, inflated sealskin float and wound plugs to prevent the loss of valuable blood.

The oldest known kayak in Britain today is in The Hull Trinity House. According to a catalogue entry, and inscription, it was acquired in 1613. 'Andrew Barker, one of the Masters of this House, on his voyage from Greenland, *Anno*

Kayaks

Domini 1613, took up this boat and a man in it of which this is the effigy.' A description by T. Gent, who published his history of Kingston upon Hull in 1735, is as follows:

> Above [the stairs] are two noble rooms:- One for the Brethren to consult their affairs, the other is the place wherein are made sails for large ships or lesser vessels. In the latter, near the ceiling, hangs a canoe or little boat covered with skins. A Groenlander is represented in Effigy sitting therein with his lower parts below deck. A pair of Oars in his right hand and a Javelin or Dart (wherewith 'tis thought he wounded the more stubborn fish) in his left. On his head seems a sort of Trencher Cap, and a bag of skins lay by him either to feed what he caught of the Finney Race, or else to contain a certain Oyl, wherewith he used to entice them. He had also with him a large Jaw Bone of a mighty Whale. Captain Andrew Barker took him upon the Sea, (in his boat with all these Implements, still preserved except the natural body, for which the Effigy is substituted) in the year 1613. But so ill did this seeming son of Neptune brook his captivity, that, refusing to eat what was kindly offered him, he died three days time.

One or two rather interesting points to note here are: Gent's reference to the 'Finney-Race'; either he was familiar with the Orkney and Shetland tradition, or else he had some other knowledge of the Fin-men; and, did he really carry with him 'a large Jaw Bone of a Mighty Whale'? This sounds like exaggeration or possibly just a misunderstanding by Gent of the circumstances of the capture. It is quite obvious that the kayak was made for a young or otherwise small person. The overall length is only a little over three and a half metres, eleven feet and nine inches. However the effigy of the person in the kayak would indicate someone of around five feet and eight inches in height, according to the upper body height from the deck line to the top of the head, which is about two feet and eight inches, or 810 millimetres. These measurements were taken during recent

Kayaks

conservation work on the kayak. Unfortunately there is no evidence of the 'Trencher Hat' reported by Gent; although the comprehensive hunting equipment and paddle appears to be complete.

We are already aware that other kayaks had appeared in Scottish waters at various times in the 17th and 18th centuries, and that sometime about 1730 an 'Eskimo' kayaker died in Aberdeen a few days after being brought ashore with his boat.

There are three 'Eskimo' type kayaks in Aberdeen, which I had the privilege to examine in September 1997; two of them are in the Anthropological Museum of Marischal College and a third in the meeting room of the Aberdeen Medico-chirurgical Society within the Foresterhill hospital complex. This last boat is in an excellent state of preservation but lacks any history to account for its arrival in Aberdeen. Its symmetrical hull and low circular cockpit suggest that it came from the South coast of West Greenland, probably from Disco Bay. This area and the opposite coast of Labrador was much frequented by Scottish whalers in the early nineteenth century. Possibly it was presented to the Society by a student or recently qualified doctor on completion of his trip to the Arctic as a ship's surgeon. It was, in any case, in their rooms by 1871. The two kayaks in the Anthropological Museum are in a much deteriorated condition but are somewhat better documented. In an inventory of Marischal College of around 1842 they are described as follows:

> Esquimaux canoe, in which a native of that country was driven ashore near Belhelvie, about the beginning of the eighteenth century and died soon after his landing.

> Esquimaux canoe with paddles, darts and other implements. Presented, 1800. by Captain William Gibbon, Aberdeen.

Kayaks

There is no direct evidence as to where either of the two kayaks originated but their shapes and profiles suggest that they, too, derive from the West coast of Greenland. The earliest reference to the kayak which came ashore near Belhelvie is by the Rev. Mr. Gastrell of Stratford-on-Avon in his account of his visit in 1760 to King's College, Old Aberdeen:

> ...In the church, which is not used, (there being a kirk for their way of worship) was a canoe about seven yards long by two feet wide which, about thirty years since was driven into the Don with a man in it who was all over hairy and spoke a language which no one could interpret.

This description is followed with suggestions as to how and why Eskimos should travel so far from home, with reference made to the reports of both Wallace and Brand. It is interesting, and a cause for consideration, that the common Orkney and Shetland term 'Finmen' is neither cited nor disputed.

Some mystery surrounds the kayak which Wallace mentions as being in the Physicians' Hall, Edinburgh, around the year 1688; as there is no positive identification of this artifact at the present time. This kayak was part of Sir Andrew Balfour's collection, which on his death in 1694, was bequeathed to the University of Edinburgh. However, it appears that the kayak remained in the Physicians' Hall, despite there being an entry in the Minute Book of the Royal College of Physicians for the 24th. of September 1696 marking the transfer to the University.

David MacRitchie was of the opinion that it may well have been with the University, though not 'officially' recorded since there seems to have been inconsistencies in the Town Council registers. He points out that when the University Museum collection was transferred to the

Kayaks

Museum of Science and Art in 1865, it contained 'ethnographical objects' which included two kayaks. In spite of this lack of documentary evidence relating to a specific kayak, MacRitchie furnishes material evidence which suggests there is sufficient difference between the two kayaks in the collection to suggest a disparate provenance.

The extensive use of baleen for ribs and various fastenings in one of the kayaks is quite significant; also the 'exceptional luxury' of a cushion made from sealskin and padded with heather. A plan view of this kayak reveals that the bow tapers finely, but with a deep forefoot, whilst towards the shallow drafted aft end the beam is continued in breadth close to the extremity – 'exceptional, if not unique'. Everything in the construction of the kayak is stitched or tied, there is no other form of fastening to be seen; which again sets it apart from the Eskimo kayaks which make extensive use of ivory pins and wooden 'treenails'. Its overall length of seventeen feet nine and a half inches is close enough to the average length of eighteen feet; whereas the greatest breadth of beam is one foot eleven inches, compared to the average of one foot six and a half inches. It is considerably heavier, weighing sixty pounds, as against the average of thirty-three and a half pounds. These 'average' measurements I have extracted from a range of thirty one specimen kayaks.

One of the six kayaks held by the National Museum of Scotland in Edinburgh is sufficiently close in its general appearance to the one described by MacRitchie, but the overall measurements are a bit different. It is described in the Museum catalogue as follows:

> The origin of this Kayak is obscure. Sir Henry Wade who became Conservator in 1903 believes it to have been in the possession of the College [Royal College of Physicians] for a long period. About the beginning of the second World War, the Kayak and much other

Kayaks

lumber in the Museum Attic was given to a junk merchant and for two or three years the Kayak was stored in a shed in Duff Street, Gorgie, Edinburgh. The merchant had had offers for it, chiefly by persons wishing to use it, and it was necessary to offer financial inducement to restore the Kayak to the College. It is not known whether any repairs were undertaken by the merchant.

The Kayak is eighteen feet long and seventeen and a half inches in maximum width. It is very light and can be readily lifted by one person. The frame-work is chiefly of pine wood and the side pieces seen through the opening show 'rip marks' of planing. The ribs and other timber are firmly bound by leather thongs. The frame is covered by skin – presumably of the seal – the seams being all above, overlapped, and doubly sewn with gut. The opening in which the Eskimo sits has a wood rim, spliced behind and made secure by a reinforcement of bone and teeth [? of the seal] used as nails. The skin covering passes under this rim and is hitched to teeth driven obliquely into the inner side of the rim. Leather thongs cross the deck in front and behind the opening to hold darts and paddles.

This description could very well be applied to most kayaks, but subtle differences in design and construction make each one quite distinctive. This particular one is exceptionally well built, and fully demonstrates an outstanding degree of skill by the maker. I would have no difficulty in identifying it as that described by MacRitchie if it were not for the conflicting dimensions. It cannot be determined visually whether the ribs are made from baleen or pine, though their slender proportions could indicate the former. There is however a repaired or spliced rib underneath the opening, confirming MacRitchie's description where he states 'the cross ribs, which appear to be about thirty in number, are of baleen, – that is, with the exception of the two which are in front of the paddler. These are of wood, and have been joined or spliced.' Despite the

Kayaks

uncertainties which obscure the positive identity of this kayak, we cannot ignore MacRitchie's comments; and certainly as far as the outward profile and plan are concerned, it is different enough for questions to be raised regarding its provenance.

The Eskimo name 'kayak' is the most familiar for this type of craft, and is indeed the commonly accepted term for the totally enclosed type of boat used by the Sealfolk. These apparently simple vessels, expertly handled by masters of the ocean, had the most extraordinary capabilities. I have already referred to John Brand's account where he states 'And when in a storm he seeth the high surge of a wave approaching, he hath a way of sinking his boat, till the wave passes over'.

There is also an interesting account by American observers, Dr. G.F. Wright and Mr. Warren Upham, albeit from Greenland, describing in 1896 what I believe refers to similar craft in the hands of a similar people:

> At one time, while in camp at Ikamiut, when the wind was blowing a gale, shutting us up all day in our tent and tossing the waves of the fjiord into such a commotion that it would have been madness for any large boat to have ventured upon the water, we were thrilled by the cry that some kayakers were coming. They were three that belonged to the little settlement, and had come that day as a matter of course from Sukkertoppen, which was twenty miles distant. Upon reaching the shore and pulling themselves loose from their shells (canoes), the kayakers ran their hands into the apertures from which they had drawn their limbs, and brought out various objects of merchandise which they had purchased at the store for their families. Then they severally took up their kayaks and carried them to a secure place, and disappeared in the igloos (huts of earth and stones), where their families soon joined them to talk over the adventures of the week. *To us they seem like inhabitants of the sea, who were accustomed to shed their skins on coming out of the water.*[My ITALICS]

Kayaks

Also from Greenland, but from the much earlier date of 1398, we have the report of Sir Nicolo Zeno in *The Discovery of the Islands of Frislandia, Eslanda, Engronelanda, Estotilanda, and Icaria* [FAIR-ISLE, ICELAND, GREENLAND, AND TWO ALTERNATIVE NAMES FOR NEWFOUNDLAND]; *Made by Two Brothers of the Zeno Family, Namely Messire Nicolo the Chevalier, and Messire Antonio. With a Map of the Said Islands* [TRANSLATED TITLE]. published in Venice, in 1558.

> The native fishermen's boats are made like unto a weaver's shuttle. Taking the skins of fishes [WALRUS HIDES], they fashion them with bones [BONE NEEDLES] of the self-same fish, and sewing them together and doubling them over, they make them so sure and substantial that it is wonderful to see how, in bad weather, they will shut themselves close inside and expose themselves to the sea and wind without the slightest fear of coming to mischief. If they happen to be driven on any rocks, they can stand a good many bumps without receiving any injury. In the bottom of the boats they have a kind of sleeve, which is tied in the middle, and when any water comes into the boat, they put it into one half of the sleeve, then closing it above with two pieces of wood and opening the band underneath, they drive the water out of the boat; and this they do as often as they have occasion.

Kreutzmann recognised the antiquity and widespread use of the kayak. 'Where there are Eskimos there are also kayaks, be it Alaska, Canada or Greenland. Even the Reindeer Eskimos in the interior of Canada had Kayaks.' Combining this knowledge with evidence of skin boats in Russia and Finland, there is ample reason to believe that the kayak was used throughout the whole of the circumpolar cultural region. MacRitchie points us to the description by the English navigator Stephen Burrough, of Samoyeds in the extreme northeast of Russia between the island of Vaigatz and the

Kayaks

mouth of the River Petchora in 1556: 'Their boats are made of deers' skins, and when they come ashore they carry their boats with them upon their backs.'

In 1653, in the same region, a member of a Danish expedition, Martinière, describes the native canoes of single and two-person types. Regarding the latter which was captured, he says:

> The canoe was made in the style of a gondola (*fait en gondolle*), being fifteen or sixteen feet long by two and a half feet broad, very cleverly constructed of fish ribs covered with fish skins stitched together, thus making the canoe a purse, as it were, from one end to the other, within it the two were enclosed up to the waist in such a manner that not a single drop of water could get into their little vessel, so that they were enabled to expose themselves to every tempest without any danger.

M. Charles Rabot refers to this account in the September 1911 edition of *La Géographie* – 'This description and the dimensions correspond very exactly to those of the two-holed kayak in use about Bering's Straits. The fish-skin is certainly seal-skin; a seal, a whale, and a walrus being equally a 'fish' to Martinière.'

If the kayak was used by the Samoyeds as far west as Ostrov Vajgac and the gulf of Pecora islands, as accounted for here, then it would be logical to assume that at least the Kola peninsula Lapps would have been familiar with this type of craft, since the Samoyed region also extended to the White Sea. In fact it seems extremely odd if the kayak was not in use throughout the whole of the circumpolar cultural area, and yet we find so many who have denied its existence within the Lapp society. In view of the widespread use of skin covered boats in the Arctic regions, I would certainly be more in favour of accepting that the Lapps used kayaks at some time in the past, at least until it can be definitely proved otherwise.

The Norwegian archaeologist Bernhard Faerøyvik, in *Inshore Craft of Norway*, discusses another type of craft

Kayaks

used by the Lapps which was known by him as the 'Scolt', although this may only imply the boats used by the Scolt Lapps. It appears to have been a transitional stage in the development from skin to wooden construction. This follows the more traditional methods of wooden 'clinker' construction, using overlapping planks or strakes. Those planks were stitched through the overlap using sinews, and were fastened with treenails to the stems and frames; they were built up to 'ottring' (eight-oared) size, and mainly fished for cod and herring. In Outer Hebrides oral tradition, a similar name – *scolp* – was applied to the vessels used by *clann 'ic Mhanuis* ; the same also is reflected in place-names.

Presumably the *scolp* were wooden boats of a Norse or Lapp type, to have been of adequate service to the Sons of Magnus. However, there is mention of skin-boats in the Hebrides, and this is borne out by the definition of the Gaelic word *curachan* in Armstrong's dictionary (1825): 'a little boat or coracle; a little skiff; a canoe'. Armstrong says that the Hebrideans 'fearlessly committed themselves, in those slight pinnaces, to the mercy of the most violent weather'.To which MacRitchie adds the comment 'Indeed, the open skin-boat would be the last kind of vessel in which one would 'fearlessly commit oneself to the mercy of the most violent weather,' although a *decked* kayak might prove safe enough.'

As mentioned earlier, the Finn-folk kayakers were endowed with quite extraordinary characteristics. The following are a few of those observations.

George Mackenzie, schoolmaster, Rathven: 'Then the man-fish dived, but rose again at some distance'. Six Shetland fishermen, 1833: 'The superstitious fishermen threw her overboard eventually, and related that she dived in a perpendicular direction'. John Brand: 'When any endeavour to approach them they flee away most swifty', 'He hath a way of sinking the boat, till the wave passes over'.

Kayaks

I believe it would be perfectly feasible for a seal-skin kayak to submerge when launched from a sitting position on a seaweed covered rock and thrust into the water. Entering the water at an angle, a few deft strokes with the paddle would increase the forward momentum, thereby increasing the distance travelled under water. This could be anything from a few metres to several 'boat-lengths' depending on the amount, or lack, of buoyancy in the kayak due to absorption of water by the skin cover; and obviously, according to the skill of the individual kayaker. Similarily, those actions referred to by Brand and Graves, also alluded to by Munro, MacKenzie, and Edmonston, where the kayaker enters an oncoming wave, or dives completely from sight, indicate the ability to submerge the kayak at will.

If we carefully consider the design and construction of a kayak it can then be seen how this unconventional characteristic becomes feasible. In the first instance the basic design allows for only minimal buoyancy, since the maximum breadth is only sufficient to accept the lower half of the body, as Kreutzmann put it, 'tailormade to the width of the hips of the owner'. The depth, from deck to keel, is also very shallow, 9 to 11 inches (230 to 280 mm.). The remainder of the hull tapers away very finely, with hollow lines towards the bow and stern. The kayak is completely decked over, apart from the opening, or manhole, which varies in shape and size, but generally no larger than is necessary to accept the occupant whose upper clothing is fitted to the rim or flange of the manhole to make a perfectly watertight seal. Therefore it can be seen that the kayak is something which is made to fit, and is to be worn like an additional garment; as distinct from a conventional boat – 'the man and the kayak become one', as W.C. Souter put it.

The rate of sea-water absorption by the seal-skin covering has been indicated by Ian Whittaker thus: 'These craft ... normally become waterlogged [i.e. the

Kayaks

skin is saturated] after about forty-eight hours in the water.' We can be quite certain that these skins were adequately preserved and treated in the best possible manner, to prolong the serviceability and integrity of the whole covering, yet despite whatever treatment was employed it was still quite normal for the skin covering to absorb water. The need for regular 'drying out' is also alluded to by John Heath. So it can be appreciated that even after a fairly short time, a considerable amount of buoyancy is forfeited simply on account of the kayak adapting to its marine environment. A further reduction in buoyancy is obvious if the kayak were sitting lower in the water, as the skin covering of the slender wood framework is acted upon by water pressure and forced inwards between the frame spaces – more so in its waterlogged state – in a series of 'hollows' on the hull. Any corresponding increase in the internal air pressure would be vented through the occupant's outer garment. In this condition of minimal buoyancy, that is, *the normal state of a kayak at sea*, it would be relatively easy to propel the kayak just under the surface, at least for short distances.

A modern plywood or fibreglass kayak would not be so disposed, retaining maximum buoyancy at all times and relatively unaffected by water ingress or external pressures. In fact it would be extremely difficult, if even possible at all, to totally submerge one willfully, unless by damage to the hull or being flooded accidentally through a leaking deck hatch , as was the experience of Robin Lloyd-Jones at the Treshnish Isles to the west of Mull.

> It was at this point that my kayak sprang a leak ... I must have taken in a hundredweight or more of water. Every time I sped down the steep front of a wave, the bows, instead of lifting again, continued on their downward trajectory. Several times I was submerged up to my chest before what little buoyancy there was asserted itself. I paddled flat out for the nearest island.

Kayaks

This one incident clearly demonstrates in a dramatic way the effects of reduced buoyancy in a modern kayak, fortunately this time in the hands of a highly skilled sea-kayaker.

One other point of interest raised first of all by Wallace, and that is the problem of how to cater for natural bodily functions. He describes the way that Finn-men are secured in their little boat – 'His fhirt he has is fo faftned to the Boat, that no Water can come into his Boat to do him damage, except when he pleafes to unty it, which he never does but to eafe nature, or when he comes afhore.'

I just cannot imagine what kind of image Wallace had of a kayaker performing the implied function, even in flat calm conditions; or worse still, the thought of Heath's discomforts during his fantastic hypothetical voyage from Greenland to Orkney – even with frequent rests on icebergs!

Amazingly, the perfect means of accomplishing these essential functions safely had been put into practice centuries before Wallace penned his own thoughts on it. In Sir Nicolo Zeno's account of 1398 describing the Greenland Eskimo and their boats, he says,

> In the bottom of the boats they have a kind of sleeve, which is tied in the middle, and when any water comes into the boat, they put it into one half of the sleeve, then closing it above with two pieces of wood and opening the band underneath, they drive the water out of the boat; and this they do as often as they have occasion.

This is obviously a very simple and effective bladder type pump, not far removed in design from what nature endowed ourselves with, and perfectly safe to operate in all but the very worst conditions. Sir Nicolo Zeno indicates its use as a bilge pump, but it is not difficult to visualise a secondary use for this ingenious contrivance. The obvious question is of course, Why did it not continue in use?

Kayaks

It apparently does not exist in any of the kayaks described by other writers, and even Gert Nooter who is an acknowledged authority on kayaks, mentions 'the elimination of waste products of the body' as one of the reasons why a kayak is not a suitable vessel in which to undertake a voyage from Greenland. Furthermore, in his description of kayaks from Greenland there is no reference to any equipment specific to ridding the kayak of bilge water or any other unwanted waste. Heath – who cautiously concedes such a voyage is possible – on the other hand disposes of the problem by stating that a kayaker would have to make a choice between 'living or having soiled trousers'!

Nooter's objection is basically grounded on the theory that kayaks are not designed for open sea voyages, 'they are boats for fjords and coastal waters', and therefore could not survive a long voyage, and that on account of becoming waterlogged they could not proceed much beyond forty-eight hours. Despite his strongly argued reasoning and support for the theory of transhipment as curiosities by whalers, he is at a loss to explain how two out of the eighteen kayaks in the Netherlands arrived on the Dutch coast. About one of these it is said that 'The city of Zierikzee is supposed to have been founded in 849 by a man named Zierik, who is said to have arrived in a kayak for that purpose.' And the other was found at sea along with the dead kayaker, from whom a piece of skin is preserved with the kayak. On those two events Nooter grudgingly surrenders to the endorsement of folklore – 'in the absence of proof we shall have to make do with the tradition.'

Nevertheless, absence of proof should not diminish the strength of evidence to hand. The very fact that those kayaks exist, and there is a robust local tradition to support their arrival or discovery should be accepted, and if not, it certainly begs the question – who then founded Zierikzee?

Kayaks

Whether or not the Sjø-Sami built and used seal-skin kayaks is an intriguing question. Many historians deny that they ever used skin boats, since all available evidence points to their expertise in the building of wooden boats. Arne Emil Christensen writes 'We know nothing of the appearance of the Lappish boats in past ages', and here he was specifically referring to wooden boats, since the earliest historical records only extend to seventeenth and eighteenth century literature. What we do know from those sources is that 'The Lapps of Northern Norway built their boats differently from the Norwegians'. The archaeologist Nicolay Nicolaysen believed it was possible there may have been a link between skin covered boats and the early planked boats of Northern Norway; and more recently Professors A.W. Brøgger and Haakon Shetelig have strongly supported this theory.

It is reasonable to assume that at some stage in the past, before those Lapps developed the tools and the skills to cut and shape thin wide boards sufficiently pliable for moulding and stitching together to form a seaworthy vessel, they would have utilised animal skins to cover a simple framework of bent wood. Although it is difficult to assess from ancient rock carvings in Northern Norway exactly how the vessels there represented were constructed, there is absolutely no doubt that some type of skin boats were in common use in North Norway, and Brøgger provides adequate justification for their existence through his own investigations combined with the expert knowledge of others who studied the evidence. He comments that 'it was the skin boat which made possible the settlement of all the western isles, the furthest outposts of Lofoten, Vaerøy, and Røst'.

Stone-age rock carvings in North Norway and the Islands depict the skin boats of that time; all similar in basic shape, with an elevated curved prow, and most of them clearly intended for use by one person. It is

Kayaks

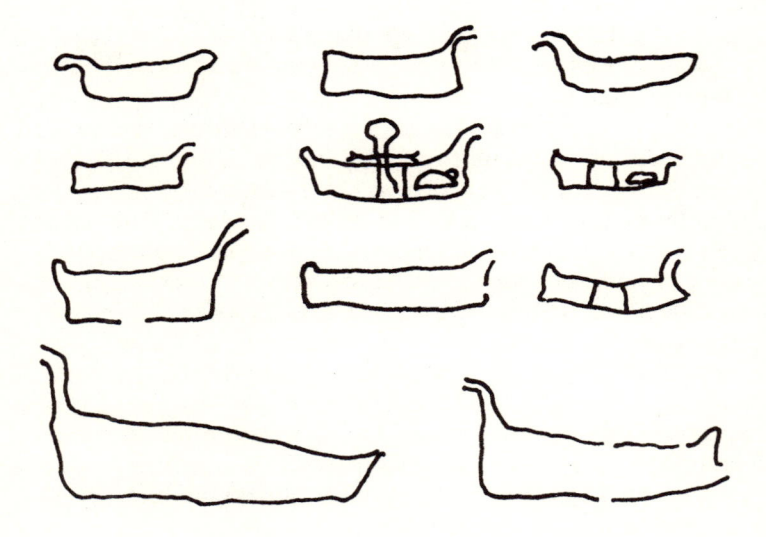

impossible to tell if any of those boats were in any way decked over with skin, as in a kayak; but vertical divisions of the hull, as seen in many of the carvings, could quite easily imply an open compartment for the occupant in the middle of the boat leaving one or both ends covered in by a watertight deck. Professor Gutorm Gjessing, whose expertise is shared with Brøgger, categorically states that the kayak never had a place in Norwegian life, and that this type of craft achieved its 'highest and most functional development' with the Greenland Eskimos.

By the time that sightings and capture of people in kayaks were recorded in Scottish history, traditional wooden boatbuilding in Norway had long passed its zenith, and continued only in the Nordland district into the beginning of this century. Even if we were to assume that the design of the Greenland kayaks had been imported and put to use by the Lapps following the Norse occupation of 'Groneland', and here again I have

Kayaks

no hesitation in suggesting the Sjø-Sami, it is quite possible that minimal usage of a particular type of boat could have existed without cause for noting its historical significance in any way.

We all know that there have been many transient contrivances and whimsical gadgets, some good and some not so good, in our own recent history which were totally obscured by subsequent technology. And after all, we must remember the very existence of the Lappish race and all they stood for was an affront to the 'civilised' Norwegians, with absolutely no obligation to learn about the people or their history. However, in view of the Lapp's known expertise in early wooden boat building, and in the methods they continued to employ up to fairly recent times, it would be perfectly safe to say that in earlier times their proficiency in the building of skin boats would undoubtedly have achieved the same high degree of natural perfection.

The design of a kayak does not allow for a lot of equipment to be carried on board apart from what was required for a particular purpose, and then only what could safely be stowed on the deck. Seal-skin straps or lanyards were built into the kayak at strategic points across the deck, in front of, and behind the manhole. Internal stowage would be very restrictive owing to the occupant pretty well filling up the manhole, and also the fastening around the deck flange would have to be undone, thus exposing the kayak to the risk of flooding by waves breaking over.

The one vital piece of ancillary equipment was of course a paddle. This was normally double ended and with very narrow blades, quite unlike the wide spoon shape of modern paddles, but yet cleverly designed to be highly effective in use, and in the hands of a skilled operator speeds of around ten to twelve knots were achievable. Likewise all the hunting equipment was economically contrived, but with the same degree of

Kayaks

perfection that only comes from many generations of experience.

The paddle, spear, bird-spear, throwing-stick, and harpoon, forming the equipment found with the Aberdeen kayak have been well described by Professor Reid, and again indicate the high level of workmanship executed in the manufacture of vital equipment. The only other essential piece of equipment normally carried on hunting trips, but not present in the Aberdeen collection, is the harpoon line and its stowage receptacle. These are adequately described by Gert Nooter, and once again demonstrate the inherent competence and practical composition of native inventiveness.

~ 7 ~

LAPP OF HONOUR

Maybe it would be quite inappropriate to furnish an easy solution to the age-old mystery of our Seal-folk and visitations by strange people in kayaks. To rob future generations of the intrigue and the delight of flirtation with the unknown would be to discharge too recklessly our vast treasure-house of folklore. Even at this time, we ourselves are creating the mysteries of tomorrow, our lives are constantly adding to the unfolding pages of human astonishment. It is now possible to exist for months in the depths of the ocean in an artificially created environment, or on board nuclear powered submarines; it is even possible for man to travel far into space, and some already have walked on the surface of the moon. Who knows, maybe in the not so distant future, people will contemplate these facts and suggest that it would have been impossible for us to have accomplished them! After all, they will say, it is only folklore.

If, at this present time, people with little or no contact with the outside world – and indeed there still are such people in remote parts – were called upon to describe an encounter with, for example, our naval 'frogmen' or modern Scuba divers in their close fitting wet-suits, I dare say the descriptive version of what they witnessed would not be far removed from what those who described the Seal-folk of only two to three hundred years ago had to say.

To be in possession of a 'skin' with apparently supernatural properties, capable of immediately transforming a perfectly normal human being into a strange sea-creature, and vice versa, is the single most powerful element presented to the innocent observer's mind. The fact that there is a particular type of boat (the

Lapp of Honour

kayak) along with its various accoutrements accompanying the 'transformed' owner, is of far less significance.

If we were to consider several familiar phenomena in our own experience, and not all of them necessarily marine related, we can more easily relate to the mystery concerning the existence of Seal-folk. Just think of how various articles of clothing, for example a particular uniform, can apparently change very ordinary people. In all cases, it is the 'skin' or special outer garment which appears to transform the person. Therefore, the visual impact of a person clothed in a certain way creates a completely new image.

How we react to encounters with such 'transformed' beings affects the way we are likely to convey our impression of that experience to others – some images we can feel comfortable with; others may be less so. Nevertheless, in all cases, the most important factor in forming that image is the 'skin'.

Return now to our kayaker, dressed overall in sleek seal-skin, whose outward shape alone betrays the real human form enclosed. The material of his indispensable garment has not undergone any process which renders it unrecognisable, or as to be anything other than the original seal-skin. The image created therefore, on visual contact, is that of some seal-like creature – albeit with a vaguely discernible human shape.

The simple fact that those Seal-folk were generally accepted by the Island people to be Finns merely following their normal pattern of social behaviour, makes it possible that in some places, at least, their appearance was so common as not to provoke undue concern or comment. And even if their use of kayaks and associated implements identified them as fellow humans; any spontaneous description of them would always be relative to the initial visual impact.

Since they were first generally reported around the beginning of the eighteenth century (and it is unlikely that there would have been written reports from the

Lapp of Honour

Islands before this time) there has been a considerable amount of research done into the mysterious circumstances by which 'Eskimo' kayaks could have arrived in this country. Notably, and almost without exception, historians have chosen to associate those kayaks with the Greenland and Labrador coastal regions.

Certainly, many of them had their origin in those areas, and there are verifiable accounts as to how and why some were taken to this country and also to the Netherlands. Whalers and sealers hunting in those regions frequently returned with 'curiousities' and these included not only kayaks but also the Eskimos themselves. Many of the exhibits in our museums arrived in this manner, and there is ample evidence to support this, even with exact details of the various expeditions and the ship's captains responsible for returning with them.

However, not all are accounted for, and particularily those which were taken at sea or captured near our coasts. In those ambiguous cases we have to rely solely on the accuracy of local oral tradition and broadly explicit folklore. So there remains this question of where, why, and how there were kayakers found in different places around our coasts, and what is the reason for so many of the Island traditions pertaining to the mysterious appearances of strange sea-creatures.

There are some who point to every single one of the kayaks having been shipped across by whalers, and imply that those which were later seen or captured were merely 'escapees' attempting to return home. It has been suggested that some were possibly released before a ship's arrival in its home port, for fear of recriminations following the great numbers of human specimens that were being exploited. A lot of this is purely conjecture and does not provide any concrete evidence which would adequately explain why there should be so many events around the same period in time.

Lapp of Honour

Voluntary crossings of the north Atlantic from Greenland via Iceland and the Faroes have variously been suggested, as well as forced voyages after being caught out at sea in severe weather and unable to return to wherever they had departed from. Various theories are presented as to how it may be possible for the voyage to be made, including the notion of riding 'piggy-back' on an iceberg. I would go as far as to say that this is even more ridiculous than some profess mythology to be. Why should an experienced 'kayaker' be content to sit it out idly on top of an iceberg which was obviously carrying him over twelve hundred miles in the wrong direction? I cannot accept that this is likely, except in a very remote case of injury or other form of distress. As to making the exceptional voluntary crossing, it cannot be ruled out as being impossible, for

Lapp of Honour

it need not be fundamentally outwith the scope of an expert and extremely fit kayaker to achieve; however, it has to be asked why indeed should anyone venture making the hazardous excursion at all?

It is interesting that some of those who profess to be experts on kayaks prefer to ignore the Seal-folk and Finn-folk lore which is common to the location of all kayak encounters. But why is there such a reluctance to associate traditional lore with those clearly physical appearances? Why should anyone isolate the evidence of specific historical events, and then arrive at a tidy practical conclusion to the riddle of the kayak, whilst dismissing entirely the enigma of the traditional element? Is it the case that it's safer to follow a line, however tenuous, of irrefutable evidence, or, did H.G. Wells correctly identify our inherent weakness, and our fear of ridicule? 'Stuff that the public won't believe aren't facts.'

If we choose to disregard the evidence of the kayaks entirely, or to categorise all of them as curiosities imported by whalers – as indeed we have to accept many of them were – there still remains the overriding question of how the Seal-folk and Finn-folk traditions originated and subsequently developed as an important aspect in the maritime cultural heritage of the Scottish Islands.

Could it be at all possible that only a tiny remnant of 'Finn' settlers from the Norse occupation period chose to remain, following the return of the Isles to Scottish rule, and continued to practise the aquatic lifestyle of their ancestors? If that were the case, then it raises an even greater controversy. Was there a mass exodus from the Islands around 1266, and if so, how were the Islands repopulated afterwards? The hypothesis is highly unlikely.

If, on the other hand, we accept that the indigenous population had socially amalgamated with the incoming dominant society, as certainly appears to have been the case if we examine the history of the Lordship of the Isles, then it is altogether feasible that an insignificant

Lapp of Honour

constituent within that society, or in modern parlance, an ethnic minority, should continue with their own hereditary culture and traditions.

This is evident in the lifestyle of many native Islanders today, especially in the more isolated districts, where hereditary traits in individual communities can be seen to dominate modern cultural trends; and this I must add, is exactly as it's seen through the eyes of a native islander.

The evidence of families living today whose traditions associate them with *sliochd nan ròn* and *na Lochlannaich* must also be taken seriously, and subjected to our fair reasoning. Native genealogists have always strictly observed fundamental characteristics in the pragmatic application of their science, enabling us today to rely solidly on the evidence of oral tradition – this is aptly illustrated in some idiosyncratic nicknames which follow generation after generation of islanders.

There was a family of MacDonalds from Heisgeir who were known as *na Lochlannaich*, Possibly the very same as were referred to in the ancient song *Clann Domhnuil 'ic a' Ròin*, Children of Donald son of the Seal, of which the first and last verses are reproduced here:

> *Bi am briomal ri bròn,*
> *Ann an Sgeirean a' Bhodh-à',*
> *Bi ròn teilich 'na chòir,*
> *Ri robhadh nan cuilean.*

> *'S a Chlann Domhnuill 'ic a' Ròin,*
> *'S iomadh òran milis,*
> *Bhite togail le sùnnt,*
> *Mu 'n cuairt air bhur tulaich.*

Sad the cry of the seal
In the rocks of the current,
Keeping watch o'er the pups
And sending them warnings.

So, you Children of the Seals,
Many songs were sweetest
When they sang them with love
In homes you're now leaving.

Lapp of Honour

There is another family line descended from Calum MacAskill or *Calum na ròn,* also from Heisgeir, who was reckoned to be the progeny of the Seal-folk, of whom many are still to be found living in the Sollas district of North Uist. Calum, who was born sometime around the latter half of the 1760s, married a Mary MacPhail from Malacleit by whom he had eight children between the years 1785 and 1821. He had settled in that district around the beginning of the nineteenth century. Many of the family descendants had emigrated to Australia during the time of the clearances, but quite a number still remain in and around the same area of North Uist. A direct descendant, Lachlann Alick MacInnes of Leicester, was able to supply me with details of the family history exactly as it was passed down from one generation to the next – accompanied by Calum's family tree of eight generations of Seal-folk!

If we now carry our thoughts across the North Atlantic, and consider the possibility that the remainder of the early Norse settlers in Greenland were to be displaced by the native Eskimos who were again recolonising the areas of land which they had once forsaken, maybe on account of drastic climatic changes, then it would be entirely possible that they would choose to backtrack the outward migration route. A return journey from Greenland via Iceland, the Faroes, Shetland, and Orkney could then provide a logical explanation for those sightings of people in kayaks in and around the Scottish islands.

Following its discovery by the Norsemen, the southern part Greenland had been colonised from Iceland from about the end of the tenth century onwards; at which time the Eskimo population lived much further to the north. In 1264 it was politically united with Norway, and by the middle of the fourteenth century there were two flourishing colonies on the south-west coast, named West Bygd and East Bygd. However, those settlements gradually disappeared, and various expeditions sent from Denmark between 1585 and 1670 were unsuccessful in locating them. Those

Lapp of Honour

expeditions would likely have formed part of the extensive whale and seal fisheries which were established from Scotland, England and the Netherlands from around 1590 onward, to exploit the rich harvest in the waters of the north-west Atlantic. The Elizabethan explorers, Sir Martin Frobisher and John Davis, 'rediscovered' the coast of Greenland during expeditions to discover a north-west passage to India; but it was in 1721 that a Danish clergyman, Hans Egede, established a new settlement called Good Hope or Godthåb which is now the capital.

So, where did the original Icelandic/Norse settlers go to from East and West Bygd, or what happened to them? Were they forced out by the re-establishment of Eskimo colonies? Would they have retraced the routes navigated by their ancestors? And did they do so in kayaks? If that was so, did they spend the next century lurking in remote parts of the Faroes, Shetland, Orkney and the Hebrides? These are important questions which if answered could lead us closer to unravelling the mystery of the Seal-folk in the Islands.

We can be almost certain that the kayak, which no doubt they would have been perfectly accustomed to, would have been the one and only means of escape available to them since there were no suitable trees for conventional boatbuilding available on Greenland. So, were those occasional sightings of kayakers descendants of the Norse people from Greenland who had chosen to stop in the Scottish Islands, rather than vagrant Eskimos as suggested? Or, did they even go all the way back to Norway, and revisit our Islands from there?

We have read Lieut.Temple's suggestion that a particular caste known as 'Strils' were said to inhabit the islands around Bergen – the part of Norway closest to Shetland. Could the Strils have been refugees from Greenland? We must also consider the possibility they may have been small parties of nomadic Finns or Lapps venturing directly from North Norway. Furthermore, we must bear in mind that they had probably already

Lapp of Honour

established themselves in the Scottish Islands during the period of Norse occupation.

We have heard the testimony of tradition and folklore, and we have heard of unmistakeably mythological events. We acknowledge the professionalism of historians, archaeologists, and specialists in the various fields of maritime research alike, who unfailingly continue to enlighten us as their own knowledge expands. Yet, there appears to be no end to the mysterious testing of our imaginations in the quest to discover the reality on which our precious heritage of oral folklore is established.

The Seal-folk are very real people whom we meet and live with in the Islands. We can tell who they are and where they come from; but in spite of this there seems to be a cultural deficiency in our attitude to the apparently paranormal – a product of 'civilisation' which prevents us from wholly accepting anything other than rational thought processes and substantiated information.

Duncan Shaw, the factor for Clanranald, obviously had no such doubt in his mind when he ordered that a proper burial be provided for that extraordinarily happy creature who so distressingly died on the seaweed strewn strand of the 'Dark Island'.

REFERENCES

The following is a list of the principal academic papers and journal articles which individually and collectively have proved to be valuable sources of information for the basis of my research. The list is by no means exhaustive, and for those interested in following any other specific line of investigation, there is ample scope for study in the fields of marine archaeology, nautical mythology, Scottish and Norwegian cultural heritage and Island folklore.

Crottet, Robert 'Children of the Wild', *Time and Tide*, November 1947.

Heath, John 'The Phantom Kayakers, a Scottish Mystery', *Sea Kayaker*, Summer 1987, pp. 15-18.

Helander, Elina 'The Sami of Norway', in *Nytt fra Norge* 1992.

Idiens, Dale 'Eskimos in Scotland: c. 1682-1924', in C. Feest (ed.) *Indians of Europe, an Interdisciplinary Collection of Essays*. Aachen, Edition Herodot, Raderverlag Forum II, 1987, pp. 161-174.

Kreutzmann, Jens 'The Greenland Kayak', in *Greenland 75*. Kgl. Gronlandske Handel.

MacFarlane, A.M. 'Sea Myths of the Hebrides', *Transactions of the Inverness Scientific Society and Field Club*, Vol. 9, 1918-25, pp. 360-390.

MacKenzie, W.C., 1905. 'Notes on the Pigmies Isle, at the Butt of Lewis, with results of the recent exploration of the "Pigmies Chapel" there', *Proceedings of the Society of Antiquaries of Scotland*, March 1905, pp. 248-258.

MacRitchie, David 'The Finn-Men of Britain', *The Archaeological Review*, Vol.4, 1889, pp. 1-26.

MacRitchie, David, *Journal of the Royal Anthropological Institute of Great Britain and Ireland*, Vol. 42, 1912, pp. 493-515.

MacRitchie, David 'Kayaks of the North Sea', *Scottish Geographical Magazine*, Vol. 28, 1912, pp. 126-133.

MacRitchie, David, 'Notes on a Finnish Boat Preserved in Edinburgh', *Proceedings of the Society of Antiquaries of Scotland*, Feb 1890, pp. 353-369.

Marischal Museum *Eskimo Kayaks in Aberdeen*.

Nooter, Gert *Old Kayaks in the Netherlands*. E.J. Brill, Leiden, 1971.

Nicolaysen, N. *Langskipet fra Gogstad ved Sandefjord*, Kristiania (Oslo) 1882.

Souter, W.C. 'The Story of our Kayak and Some Others', Presidential address to the Aberdeen Medico-Chirurgical Society. The University Press, Aberdeen, 1934.

Storey, A. *Trinity House of Kingston upon Hull*, Vol. 2, 1969, p.161.

Whitaker, Ian 'The Scottish Kayaks and the 'Finn-men'', *Antiquity*, June 1954, pp.99-104.

Wright, Dr.G.F. and Upham, Warren *Greenland Icefields*, London, 1896, pp. 143-4.

Selected Bibliography

Annandale, Nelson: *The Faroes and Iceland* (1905)
Anderson, Sheila: *Seals* (1990)
Anson, Peter F.: *Fisher Folk-Lore* (1965)
Atkinson, Robert: *Shillay and the Seals* (1980)
Bennett, Alfred Gordon: *Focus on the Unknown* (1953)
Benwell, Gwen & Waugh, A.: *Sea Enchantress* (1961)
Bonner, W. Nigel: *The Natural History of Seals* (1989)
Brand, John: *A New Description of Orkney, Zetland, Pightland Firth and Caithne s* (1701)
Brøgger, A.W. & Shetelig, H. *The Viking Ships, their Ancestry and Evolution* (1951)
Brondsted, Johannes: *The Vikings* (1960)
Brown, George MacKay: *The Ocean of Time*
Carmichael, Alexander: *Carmina Gadelica* (1900)
Christensen, Arne Emil: *Boats of the North* (1968)
Craigie, William A.: *Scandinavian Folklore* (1896)
Debes, Lucas: *History of the Faroes* (1676)
Duben, Baron von: *Lappland* (1873)
Faerøyvik, Bernhard: *Inshore Craft of Norway* (1979)
Fergusson, Donald A.: *The Hebridean Connection* (1984)
Fergusson, Donald A.: *From the Farthest Hebrides* (19??)
Fisher, James: *Rockall* (1965)
Gordon, Seton: *The Immortal Isles* (1926)
Greenhill, Dr Basil: *The Archaeology of Boats and Ships – an Introduction* (1995)
Guerber, H.A.: *Myths of the Norsemen* (????)
Hibbert, Samuel: *A Description of the Shetland Isles* (1822)
Jackson, A.: *The Faroes: the Faraway Islands* (1991)
Kauffmann, F. *Northern Mythology* (1851)
Lloyd-Jones, Robin: *Argonauts of the Western Isles* (1989)
MacFarlane, A.M.: *Sea Myths and Lore of the Hebrides* (1925)
MacGregor, A.A. *The Peat Fire Flame* (1937)
Macintosh, James A.: *Rockall* (1946)
MacKenzie, W.C.: *The Western Isles* (1932)
MacNeil, F. Marion: *The Silver Bough* (1957)
MacPherson, J.M.: *Primitive Beliefs in the North-East of Scotland* (1929)
MacRitchie, David: *Testimony of Tradition* (1890)
Magnusson, E.: *The Heimskringla*, Volume 4, in 'The Saga Library', Volume 6 (1905)

Magnusson, E.: *Notes on Shipbuilding and Nautical Terms of Old in the North* (1906)

Marmele, Ernest W.: *The Folklore of Orkney and Shetland* (1975)

Martin, Martin: *A Description of the Western Islands of Scotland* (1716)

Matheson, William: *The Songs of John MacCodrum* (1938)

Millar, Hugh: *Scenes and Legends of the North of Scotland* (1855)

Moireasdan, Padruig: *Ugam agus Bhuam* (1977)

Nansen: *In Northern Mists* (1911)

Nelson, H.H. Grayburn and B. Stephen Strong: *Circumpolar Peoples: An Anthropological Perspective* (1973)

Nooter, G.W.: *Life and Survival in the Arctic* (1984)

Petersen, H.C.: *Skinboats of Greenland* (1985)

Prins, A.H.J.: *A Handbook of Sewn Boats.* (Maritime Monographs and Reports, No. 59, Maritime Museum, Greenwich)

Saxby, Jessie M.E.: *Shetland Traditional Lore* (1932)

Severin, Tim: *The Brendan Voyage* (1978)

Spencer, Bill: *Harpoponed – The Story of Whaling* (1980)

Thomson, David: *The People of the Sea* (1954)

Tudor, J.R.: *The Orkneys and Shetland* (1883)

Wallace, James: *Description of the Isles of Orkney* (1693)

Wells, H.G.: *The Sea Lady* (1902)

Williamson, Duncan: *Tales of the Seal People* (1992)